THE GREAT BIG BURGER BOOK

THE GREAT BIG BURGER BOOK

100 New and Classic Recipes for Mouthwatering Burgers Every Day Every Way

Jane Murphy | Liz Yeh Singh

Photography by Duane Winfield

The Harvard Common Press ◎ Boston, Massachusetts

The Harvard Common Press
535 Albany Street
Boston, Massachusetts 02118
www.harvardcommonpress.com

Printed in the United States of America

Printed on acid-free paper

Library of Congress Cataloging-in-Publication Data

Murphy, Jane
The great big burger book : 100 new and classic recipes for mouthwatering burgers every day every way / Jane Murphy and Liz Yeh Singh.
p. cm.
ISBN 1-55832-246-9 (hc) — ISBN 1-55832-247-7 (pbk)
1. Cookery (Meat) 2. Hamburgers. 3. Meat substitutes. I. Singh, Liz Yeh. II. Title.

TX749 .M937 2003
641.6'6—dc21

2002015395

Special bulk-order discounts are available on this and other Harvard Common Press books. Companies and organizations may purchase books for premiums or resale, or may arrange a custom edition, by contacting the Marketing Director at the address above.

10 9 8 7 6 5 4 3 2

Book design by Richard Oriolo
Cover design by Night & Day Design
Cover and interior photographs by Duane Winfield

To Jerry and Ravi—
husbands extraordinaire and the two guys
who willingly downed all the burgers, watched
familiar surroundings transformed into test kitchens,
withstood on-the-spot grilling of the questioning kind,
and responded with their own flavor takes and
critiques—we offer hugs and kisses
and, of course, leftovers.

Contents

Introduction

From its national debut at the 1904 World's Fair in St. Louis, the humble hamburger has become an American culinary icon. It's what makes McDonald's arches golden. It's the saving grace of parents short on time and college students short on skill. It's also the staple of every Fourth of July barbecue. Whether you're a red-meat lover or a devoted vegetarian, there's a burger for you: filet mignon, turkey, tofu, black bean, tuna—the list is endless.

Nothing dominates menus across the United States like the burger. It has spawned legions of famous burger joints, from the fabled Fatburger in Hollywood to Poppy's Grill in New Orleans to New York City's Jackson Hole. Americans can't stop their craving for this popular comfort food. In fact, *The Dictionary of American Food and Drink* says that the average American eats 3 hamburgers per week. That adds up to about 38 billion burgers a year, or 3 out of every 5 sandwiches we eat.

Sandwich, you gasp? Yes, the hamburger is, at its core, a sandwich. *The American Heritage Dictionary* defines it as "a sandwich made with a patty of ground meat, usually in a roll or bun." But the definition of a burger is a loose one. In these anticarbohydrate days, more Americans than ever are leaving the buns behind (so to speak). So a burger doesn't necessarily mean a whole sandwich—it can be just the patty itself.

The hamburger is the most democratic of dishes. It's that pure American invention that offers something for everyone. Choose your protein—fish, turkey, chicken, or veggie. Burgers can be made ahead and kept in the fridge, ready for last-minute cooking. They freeze well—the perfect solution when you don't want to cook or go out or even think about what to make. And there's a burger for every meal of the day. Try Snapper Hash Burgers for brunch. Think Spicy Black Bean Burgers for lunch. Sit down to Chicken Marsala Burgers for dinner. Make mini-burgers and serve them as a fun appetizer or first course. Burgers are one of the most user-friendly dishes you'll ever make.

Counting calories? Make burgers from fish, poultry, or veggies and tempt your taste buds with Grilled Mustard-Dill Turkey Burgers or Salmon Burgers in Grape Leaves. Our Juicy Portobello Burgers with Mesclun are so rich and meaty, you might not think they're vegetarian. And if you broil, grill, or even steam your burgers, there's no additional fat.

Bored with the same old burger served up with ketchup? Serve your burgers ethnic style. Head south of the border with our Guacamole Burgers with Spicy Chili Con Queso or try our Asian Tuna Burgers. Dig into our Italian-inspired Tuscan Turkey Burgers or go Greek and bring down the frat house with our Hellenic Lamb Burgers.

If you're feeling fancy, you can take it uptown with chef Reed Hearon's decadent Rich Man's Hamburger, or try our very own Duck Burgers with Wild Rice Pancakes. Impress your guests with elegant and luxurious Lobster Burgers with Hearts of Palm and Sauce Verte. No matter how you serve it, the burger is delicious in all its incarnations.

Incredible as it sounds, we know that man (and woman) cannot live by burgers alone, so we've created a cornucopia of toppings and sauces to go with your burgers. Choose Fiesta Corn Salsa, Wasabi Mayo, or Balsamic Tomato Glaze; make your own Kick-Ass Ketchup from scratch; or cool your heels with Cucumber Mint Sauce or Carrot Daikon Slaw. There's a menu of possibilities.

We hope you find *The Great Big Burger Book* indispensable. Armed with this arsenal of recipes, you can turn your meals into something extraordinary. And feel free to invent your own burgers, mixing and matching burgers and toppings to suit your tastes and cravings. Go ahead, beef up your burger repertoire and get cooking!

"You can find your way across this country using burger joints the way a navigator uses stars....We have munched Bridge burgers in the shadow of the Brooklyn Bridge and Cable burgers hard by the Golden Gate, Dixie burgers in the sunny South and Yankee Doodle burgers in the North....We had a Capitol burger—guess where? And so help us, in the inner courtyard of the Pentagon, a Penta burger."

Charles Kuralt

Burger Basics

Folks know a good burger when they see and taste one. It's easy to make and great to eat—if you follow a few simple rules. Here are some key burger tips that separate the hacks from the pros.

Cooking the Perfect Burger

- Don't fuss with the burger mixture. The less you handle it, the juicier and more tender your burger will be. Mix the ingredients together until just combined.
- Form the patty gently between your hands. This is not a stress ball—don't knead the mixture, pack it too tightly, or pummel it. TLC is good for a burger—feel the love! You can also use a mold, but we like to form it by hand to have more control over the shape.
- Accept your burger for what it is. Like people, burgers come in different sizes. Some burgers have lots of add-ins and are hefty. Others, particularly some seafood and veggie varieties, are delicate and simply won't hold together if they are too large. Some burgers have ethnic origins that dictate they get formed into smaller shapes or eaten in smaller portions. Sometimes a burger's shape and thickness are simply a matter of choice.
- Weigh the cooking pros and cons. We think nothing beats an outdoor grill when it comes to cooking burgers. But a cast-iron-skillet also will do an awesome job. A regular skillet is good—especially for delicate fish and veggie burgers or for burgers that are simmered in sauce—but avoid grill pans, which make dry burgers and don't sear well. Broiling is also a good alternative to grilling.

THE GREAT BURGER TIME LINE

1200–1500 **Tartars from Russia create steak tartare—the earliest form of the burger. These nomads enjoyed raw beef that was tenderized under their saddles as they rode.** 1400s ***Fikadelles*** **enjoyed in northern Europe. Minced beef dishes were gourmet items in 15th-century Europe. The** ***Fikadelle*** **was a German version, with**

As for grilling—charcoal or gas? There are pros and cons to each. Charcoal wins hands down for flavor. And with charcoal, you can easily add aromatic woods directly to the fire. Charcoal fires are also hotter, so burgers sear and cook up quickly. The downside, however, is the fuss: messing with briquettes, lighter fluid, and matches; waiting for the grill to heat up; and cleaning up dirty ashes. With gas, you get instant gratification: a quick fire and no messy cleanup, both big timesavers. But these grills don't hold a fire to the flavor you get from charcoal.

- Preheat your grill or skillet. It should be nice and hot before you add the burger. Give it time to heat up. This will save you cooking time, ensure a nice crust, and keep the flavors in the burger.
- Don't smash the patty! Your burger will thank you for not putting pressure on it. Pressing down on it while you cook it will only make the juices flow out—a sure-fire ticket to a dry hockey puck. And smashing doesn't speed up the cooking time much either.
- Flip your burger only once. Flipping it back and forth will dry it out without cooking it through. Plus, it might fall apart if it's big enough.

BEYOND THE MODEL T AND LIGHT BULB

Everyone knows that Henry Ford was a carmaker and that Thomas Edison invented the light bulb, but here's a little-known fact: together they invented the charcoal briquette. Ford sold the invention to E. G. Kingsford, who produced it commercially.

fried chopped meat. 1700–1800 **Hamburger gets its name and crosses the Atlantic. German sailors from Hamburg who traveled to Russia adopted the recipe for steak tartare and brought it back home. An inventive cook put it over a flame and turned it into Hamburg steak. German immigrants introduced a chopped and broiled version to the United States.** 1836 **Ten-cent Hamburg steak is most expensive item on first ➔**

How Do You Like Your Burger?

To us, a perfect burger is pink and juicy in the middle, which is somewhere between medium rare and medium. But others believe the way to heaven is through a beef burger that's blood red in the center. For safety reasons, we give cooking times for a medium burger. Not your style? Hey, it's a free country—you choose the degree of doneness.

HERE'S WHAT TO LOOK FOR TO GET THE BURGER YOU WANT

RARE **(Beef and lamb only)**	**Center is reddish pink and very soft to the touch; juices run reddish pink.**
MEDIUM RARE **(Beef and lamb only)**	**Center is quite pink and a bit firmer to the touch but still soft; juices run pink.**
MEDIUM **(Beef, lamb, pork, veal, and poultry)**	**Center is gray-white and firm to the touch; juices run clear.**
MEDIUM WELL **(Beef, lamb, pork, veal, and poultry)**	**Meat is uniformly gray and is firm to the touch; less juicy.**
WELL DONE **(Beef, lamb, pork, and poultry)**	**Meat is gray and dry and very firm to the touch.**

Seafood burgers should be cooked until just opaque through to the center.

THE GREAT BURGER TIME LINE

U.S. printed menu. Delmonico's restaurant in New York City charged only 4 cents for a beefsteak and 12 cents for a full dinner but priced its Hamburg steak at the princely sum of 10 cents. 1885 Fifteen-year-old Wisconsin lad invents American version of hamburger. Some claim it was 15-year-old Charlie Nagreen of

Safe Cooking

For the record, we must tell you that you run the risk of food contamination by eating a ground meat burger that is not cooked to medium. Those who are especially young or old or who have compromised immune systems should definitely have their burgers cooked well done.

The USDA recommends cooking beef, pork, and lamb burgers to an internal temperature of 160°F, which is 10° to 15° higher than most restaurant chefs would probably cook your burger.

Chicken and turkey burgers should be cooked thoroughly but don't need the bejesus cooked out of them to prevent salmonella poisoning. The bacteria are eradicated at 165°F.

We also like our seafood burgers just done. That means remove them from the heat just as the fish turns opaque all the way through. Overcook them and you may end up with rubbery lumps. Cook them to an internal temperature of 135°F.

To check internal temperature, use an instant-read meat thermometer.

USDA RECOMMENDED COOKING TEMPERATURES

PROTEIN	MEDIUM RARE	MEDIUM	WELL DONE
Ground turkey and chicken	**Not recommended**	**165°F**	**170°F**
Ground beef, veal, lamb, and pork	**Not recommended**	**160°F**	**170°F**

Seymour, Wisconsin, who invented the American hamburger, delivering it from his ox-drawn concession stand at the Outagamie County Fair. 1904 **Burger makes national debut at World's Fair. The St. Louis World's Fair was the first national stage for the hamburger.** 1916 **Hamburger bun is born. J. Walter Anderson, a short-order cook and founder (along with Billy Ingram) of White Castle, created the first →**

Safe Handling and Storage

Have you ever had food poisoning? The kind that forced you to spend the night bowing to the porcelain god? You have? Well, then you know why we included this section. It's a scary fact: most food poisoning cases are caused by poor handling and storage of ingredients. You could buy the best ground sirloin for a burger, but if you thaw it on the counter for several hours, it could be "game over" before you even take your first bite of the cooked burger. Here are some basic food safety rules to consider before you begin your burger binge.

HANDLING GROUND PROTEIN

- Always wash your hands, countertops and cutting boards, and cooking utensils with hot water and detergent before and after you cook, especially when you're handling ground protein. You'd be shocked at the number of people who don't bother, leaving a trail of contamination around their kitchen.

  Not yet convinced? Know this: there is a higher risk of food contamination with ground protein than with other cuts of meat. Why? Because the surface bacteria on a big piece of protein—whether it's a slab of beef or a fish fillet—are easily killed once it's cooked. The inside is not at risk because it's not exposed to the bacteria. But with ground protein, the bacteria that contaminated the outside surface are much more likely to get mixed up with the inside, especially

THE GREAT BURGER TIME LINE

hamburger bun. 1921 White Castle arrives. The first White Castle, later to become the world's first hamburger chain, opened in Wichita, Kansas. 1934 Wimpy Grills chain is launched. Inspired by the cartoon character J. Wellington Wimpy, Popeye's mustachioed pal, Wimpy's was the first chain to expand overseas.

when patties are formed. That's why the USDA recommends higher cooking temperatures for ground meat and meat mixtures than for other cuts of protein.

- Cut the risk of food-borne illness by buying a top-quality product and having it ground to order or grinding it yourself at home, provided your own equipment is spot-on clean.

"Sacred cows make the best hamburger."
Mark Twain

- Keep raw burgers in the refrigerator until cooking time. Temperature control is probably the most crucial factor in proper food handling. Keep your food out of the danger zone (40° to 140°F), where bacteria thrive. Keep cold foods below 40°F and hot foods above 140°F. Some burgers must be refrigerated to firm up before cooking; the recipe will tell you. If you want to make your burgers a few hours ahead of time, place them on a baking sheet lined with waxed paper and cover them with plastic wrap. Refrigerate until you're ready to cook them.

- Don't put the cooked burgers on the same plate with the raw ones. Talk about defeating the purpose! You could be contaminating your cooked burgers. Also, if you've put all the burgers on to cook at once, make sure to wash the plate well in hot soapy water before using it for your cooked burgers.

1948 First drive-through opens. Harry and Esther Snyder of Baldwin Park, California, opened In-N-Out Burger, the first drive-through stand with 2-way speaker boxes and carhops. 1954 Burger King opens its first operation in Miami. James McLamore and David Edgerton cofounded Burger King and sold their broiled hamburgers for 18 cents. 1955 Ray Kroc opens the first McDonald's in Des Plaines, Illinois. Kroc named his →

STORING GROUND PROTEIN

Refrigerators should be set at 40°F or lower to prevent food from spoiling and bacteria from growing. Freezers should be set at 0°F.

Raw Protein

- Ground fish, fowl, and meat are highly perishable and do not keep well in the refrigerator. Wrap well and don't let them sit for more than 24 hours. Keep raw fish no longer than 24 hours, preferably on a bed of ice, until you're ready to use it. Use vegetable patty mixtures that contain raw eggs within 24 hours.
- Freeze raw ground protein for a longer shelf life. Wrap it well in plastic, then in aluminum foil.
- Try not to keep frozen ground meat, poultry, or fish for more than 1 month. Ground meat and poultry can keep for up to 3 months if your freezer is very cold (0°F), but it will lose taste and texture. Try to use frozen ground fish within 1 month if the fish is lean. If it's a fatty fish, such as salmon, freeze it for only 1 week.

Cooked Protein

- Allow the burgers to cool, then wrap them well in plastic. Cooked meat and poultry can last for 3 to 5 days in the refrigerator, if they're stored below 40°F. Don't keep cooked fish in the fridge for more than 2 days.

THE GREAT BURGER TIME LINE

establishment after Dick and Mac McDonald's quick-serve hamburger joint in California. 1963 **Banner year for McDonald's. Ray Kroc served up his one billionth burger live on *The Art Linkletter Show*. The same year, the 500th student graduated from McDonald's Hamburger University.** 1970s **Burger chains grab big chunk**

- Freezing extends the life of your cooked burgers. Wrap them well in plastic, then aluminum foil. Meat and poultry burgers can keep in a very cold freezer (0°F) for up to 3 months. Don't freeze fish burgers for more than 1 month. Cooked veggie burgers can be frozen for up to 6 months.

THAW SMARTLY

There are three general ways to thaw protein without compromising safety or texture.

1. Place the frozen ground protein in a bowl or on a baking sheet and thaw it in the refrigerator. This can take from several hours up to 1 day.
2. Seal the frozen protein in a plastic bag and place in cool—not warm—water. Weight it down and change the water if the temperature exceeds 40°F. This method will take several hours in the fridge.
3. Microwave it. This is the fastest method, but we're not crazy about it only because we find that the outside gets cooked by the time the inside is defrosted.

Some people like to place the frozen protein in a plastic bag under warm running water. Yes, it's definitely faster, but we don't recommend it, because too often you end up with grayish meat on the outside while the center is still frozen solid. This practice also can change the flavor.

Never refreeze previously frozen protein, whether raw or cooked.

of dining-out revenue. In the late 1970s, McDonald's, Burger King, Wendy's, and Hardee's together accounted for up to 37 cents of every dollar Americans spent eating out. 1995–present **Burgers are America's favorite food. In 1995, 86 percent of the population ordered the ubiquitous patty.**

Grinding Your Own Meat

It's a lot easier to ask your butcher to do this, but for those of you who insist on knowing what goes into your ground meat, this is the method for you.

Get a meat grinder or a KitchenAid mixer with a grinder attachment. Or use a food processor, which results in more of a chopped, rather than a ground, texture.

Make sure the blades are really sharp. Then make sure all your equipment is scrupulously clean: scald it with boiling water. Refrigerate the equipment for at least 30 minutes before using. This will help keep the meat from sticking to it.

If you're using a meat grinder or grinder attachment, fit it with the ¼-inch blade. Slice the meat into 1-inch-thick strips. *Do not remove the fat.*

Now, cut the meat into ¾-inch chunks. Place the meat in the bowl of a food processor, never filling it more than half full. Pulse the meat until you achieve the texture you want.

Follow these burger ABCs and you're on your way to becoming a brilliant burgermeister.

Classic Beef Burgers with Kick-Ass Ketchup ⚙ Guacamole Burgers with Spicy Chili Con Queso ⚙ Barbecue Cheese Burgers ⚙ Korean Bulgogi Burgers ⚙ Pampas Burgers with Chimichurri Sauce ⚙ Rich Man's Hamburger ⚙ Burgers Diane ⚙ The Big Mock with Our Own Special Sauce ⚙ Barbecued Ropa Vieja Burgers with Escabeche

Where's the Beef (and Pork

Spice Rub That Cures ⚙ Jonathan Waxman's Hamburgers ⚙ Jerry's Best Beef Burgers ⚙ Sloppy Joe Burgers ⚙ Cuban Frita Burgers ⚙ Taco Burgers ⚙ Pizza Burgers ⚙ Texas-Style Beef Burgers with Pinto Beans, Bacon, and Green Chiles (aka Knife-and-Fork Burgers) ⚙ Salisbury Steak Burgers ⚙ M. F. K. Fisher–Inspired Burgers ⚙ Guinness Pub Burgers ⚙ Mark Peel's Gorgonzola Hamburgers on Nancy Silverton's Hamburger Buns ⚙ Late-Night Beef Burger with Cheddar, Horseradish, and Onion ⚙ Bulgarian

Burgers ◌ Meat Loaf Burgers with Tangy Tomato Sauce ◌ Swedish Meatball Burgers ◌ Grilled Maple Mustard Pork Burgers ◌ Honey Mustard Pork Burgers on Cheddar Thyme Biscuits ◌ Chop Suey Burgers ◌ North Carolina Chopped Barbecued Pork Burgers ◌ Andouille Bayou Burgers with Red Pepper Mayo ◌ Teriyaki Ham Burgers

and Veal and Lamb) Burgers

with Grilled Ginger Pineapple ◌ Spicy Tofu and Pork Burgers ◌ Seekh Kebab Burgers ◌ Fog City Grilled Lamb Burgers with Tomato Mint Chutney and Roasted Bell Pepper Chow-Chow ◌ Hellenic Lamb Burgers with Eggplant Feta Salad ◌ Kofte Kebab Burgers with Cucumber Mint Sauce ◌ Home on the Range Buffalo Burgers with Brooklyn Ketchup ◌ Bettah Buttah Burgers

Remember the most incredible meal you've ever had? Was it a succulent prime rib or juicy char-grilled steak? Perhaps it was a tender butterflied lamb or crisp pork roast that brought you to your knees. Or could it simply have been a flame-broiled burger? Chances are, meat played a starring role. It's substantial and always rises to the importance of the occasion. Think about it: who eats salad to celebrate a big promotion?

Have a Cow

There is no doubt that beef is America's favorite meat. We eat 76 million servings of it every day. And why not? It's an excellent source of iron, vitamin B12, zinc, and protein.

Although Americans still crave the juicy, potent flavor of beef, in reality we're eating less of it and choosing leaner cuts. Beef consumption overall has declined in recent years as we have become more health conscious.

But hold on. Ground beef is bucking the trend: sales keep climbing, and now ground beef accounts for nearly half of all beef sold today. We, of course, like to think this means people are eating more burgers.

Oink, Oink!

Beef wasn't always America's favorite meat. For hundreds of years, pork was the most popular choice. We can thank the Spanish explorers for introducing it to the New World.

Americans eat about 50 pounds of pork a year per person, including ham, bacon, and sausage. And it's not the same pork your grandma ate. Pigs are now much svelter, containing half the fat they had 30 years ago.

That pesky trichina parasite is no longer the problem it used to be, and cooking pork to 137°F will kill it. So there's no need to overcook your burger for safe eating.

Veal-ly Delicious

Veal comes from a calf less than three months old. Despite the fact that some folks avoid veal because of the conditions in which it's raised, many people continue to eat it, drawn to its delicate flavor and melting tenderness. If you're concerned about growing conditions, there are farms that raise calves in humane conditions, and many supermarkets and butchers buy their products. Look for the American Humane Association's standard "Free Farmed" label.

Baaa-shful

We're a bit more sheepish when it comes to lamb, usually saving it for special occasions. Folks often want to know the difference between lamb and mutton. Lamb is more tender and delicate and is from a sheep less than a year old. Mutton is from an older sheep and has a bolder, stronger flavor. Look for mutton in ethnic markets, particularly Greek and Indian.

As for spring lamb, nowadays it's basically a marketing tool, though spring lamb used to mean lamb produced between March and October. It's promoted for freshness and quality, but the truth is, it really doesn't taste any different from lamb born at any other time of year.

WHERE'S THE BEEF FAT?

You might be surprised to know that dark meat chicken is higher in fat than some cuts of beef.

Which Cut of Meat?

For beef burgers, our favorite cuts are ground sirloin, round, and chuck. Sirloin generally contains less fat than round or chuck, but all make very flavorful burgers. For veal burgers, choose shoulder or shank cuts.

For pork and lamb burgers, we prefer shoulder cuts. They are tougher cuts of meat, with more connective tissue and a coarser grain, but when ground, they make great burgers.

Remember, fat is flavor. That means you want your burger meat to contain between 15 and 20 percent fat. The fat actually bastes the lean meat as the burger cooks, melting as it heats up. Too little fat and you get a dry, tasteless burger. Too much fat isn't a big problem because, by law, USDA-approved ground meat cannot contain more than 30 percent fat.

Meat Quality

Here's what to look for in quality meat:

- COLOR: Generally, the older the animal, the darker the meat color. Always avoid splotchy meat.
  - Beef should be an even, rosy to purplish (older beef) red color.
  - Veal, humanely raised, should be pink or light pink.
  - Lamb can range from cherry red to darker if it's mutton.
  - Pork should be pale pink, not gray or watery looking.

FAT RULES

Ground beef can't contain more than 30 percent fat by law. New nutrition labeling requires that it be labeled 30 percent fat ground beef at the grocery store.

- **TEXTURE:** Generally speaking, good meat is smooth, with a fine grain.
- **MARBLING:** Quality beef has good marbling, which means that there are evenly distributed flecks of fat throughout the meat. For all meat, the external fat should be white, not yellow.
- **SMELL:** Meat should smell fresh—never sour, never funky.

All meat is subject to state and federal inspection and must meet quality standards. It does not have to be USDA approved, which costs extra. Yes, you are paying more for that little purple stamp that ensures you are getting a quality product.

The USDA has eight grades for beef. The top four grades are prime, choice, select, and standard. The higher the grade, the more marbling the beef has. Prime is harder to get because it is usually reserved for upscale restaurants and butcher shops. Most of what's available at the market is choice, select, or standard.

The best-quality veal usually goes to restaurants. Most of what you'll find at your supermarket is choice or good; however, veal is rarely graded, so buy your favorite brand.

Lamb is graded similarly to beef: prime, choice, good, utility, and cull. Again, prime is hard to get; most markets offer choice. Marbling always improves the taste and texture of meat, but it's not as crucial for lamb.

Most pork isn't graded, although it is subject to state and federal inspection. Some pork is graded by number, based on the ratio of lean to fat. USDA 1 is the leanest; USDA 4 is the fattest.

The Choice Is Yours

Remember, our recipes are just a guide. You don't have to use all beef just because a recipe calls for it. Try mixing it up. Combine pork and veal, or lamb and beef, or pork—even pork sausage—and lamb. Like life, your burger is what you make of it.

CLASSIC BEEF BURGERS WITH KICK-ASS KETCHUP

MAKES 4 BURGERS

Nothing beats a juicy beef burger bursting with flavor. In this recipe, it's all about the beef, so we've kept the spices to a minimum.

1½ pounds ground beef sirloin, round, or chuck, or half ground sirloin and half ground round

Salt and coarsely ground black pepper to taste

1. Form the beef into 4 patties, each about 1 inch thick. Season on both sides with salt and pepper.
2. Lightly oil the grill or a skillet over medium-high heat and cook the burgers to the desired degree of doneness, 3 to 4 minutes per side for medium rare.

SERVE IT UP on toasted sesame seed buns

TOP IT OFF with Kick-Ass Ketchup (recipe follows)

WORLD'S LARGEST KETCHUP BOTTLE

In 1949, ketchup maker Brooks Foods of Collinsville, Illinois, built a big water tower topped with a 70-foot Brooks Tomato Catsup bottle. The water tower held 100,000 gallons of water, which was used to make ketchup.

Kick-Ass Ketchup

MAKES 1 CUP

Once you've tasted this roasted tomato ketchup, you'll never want to go back to the stuff in a squeeze bottle.

2 pounds ripe plum tomatoes, halved and seeded

3 tablespoons canola oil

1 large onion, finely chopped

4 cloves garlic, minced

3 tablespoons cider vinegar

2 tablespoons firmly packed light brown sugar

½ teaspoon ground allspice

¼ teaspoon ground cumin

¼ teaspoon ground nutmeg

1. Preheat the oven to 350°F.
2. In a large mixing bowl, toss the tomatoes with 1 tablespoon of the oil until well coated. Place cut side down on a baking sheet and roast until the tomatoes are wrinkled and soft, about 30 minutes.
3. Remove the tomatoes from the oven and transfer to a food processor. Pulse until pulpy, leaving small chunks. Do not puree.
4. In a medium-size skillet, heat the remaining 2 tablespoons oil over medium heat. Add the onion and garlic and cook, stirring, until softened, 5 to 6 minutes. Add the tomato, vinegar, brown sugar, and spices and cook, stirring occasionally, until thickened, 25 to 30 minutes.
5. Let cool, then chill before using. Will keep, tightly covered, in the refrigerator for up to 1 week.

GUACAMOLE BURGERS WITH SPICY CHILI CON QUESO

MAKES 4 BURGERS

Did you know that an avocado is actually a one-seeded berry? This south-of-the-border burger mixes the guacamole into the hamburger meat for extra-rich butteriness. If you like, leave in half the jalapeño seeds for tongue-tingling heat.

1 pound ground beef round

1 small red onion, finely diced

½ cup loosely packed fresh cilantro leaves, coarsely chopped

2 tablespoons soy sauce

1 fresh jalapeño chile pepper, seeded and finely diced

1 large egg, beaten

1 small, ripe avocado, peeled, pitted, and cut into ½-inch dice

1. Mix all the ingredients except the avocado together in a large mixing bowl until well combined. Gently fold in the avocado, then form the mixture into 4 patties, each about ½ inch thick.
2. Lightly oil the grill or a skillet over medium-high heat and cook the burgers to the desired degree of doneness, 2 to 4 minutes per side for medium rare.

SERVE IT UP on toasted sesame seed buns

TOP IT OFF with a generous dollop of Spicy Chili Con Queso (recipe follows)

Spicy Chili Con Queso

MAKES 4 CUPS

This is also great as a dip for tortilla chips.

2 tablespoons unsalted butter

1 large onion, chopped

2 cups drained canned peeled tomatoes, chopped and drained well again (see Note)

1 cup canned black beans, rinsed and well drained

10 ounces extra-sharp cheddar cheese, diced

1 teaspoon chipotle chile powder

½ teaspoon ground cumin

In a large saucepan, melt the butter over medium heat. Add the onion and cook, stirring, until softened, 5 to 7 minutes. Stir in the tomatoes, beans, cheese, chipotle powder, and cumin, stirring constantly until the cheese is completely melted. Serve immediately.

NOTE Make sure to drain the tomatoes well, or the chili will be runny.

UNCLE SAM WAS A MEATPACKER

Sam Wilson, a New York meatpacker, was nicknamed "Uncle Sam" by his employees, after the "U.S." stamped on the meat containers Wilson delivered to the armed services during the War of 1812.

BARBECUE CHEESE BURGERS

MAKES 6 BURGERS

You know exactly where the beef is with these big, juicy eight-ounce burgers. We use ground sirloin for the best, beefiest flavor, but ground chuck will work just fine. By mixing the sauce in with the meat, you get the barbecue in the burger before it even hits the grill.

"Cheese and burger must have time to get acquainted and to synergize in such a way that the cheese melts and runs down the side of the burger like lava down the slopes of Vesuvius."

Ralph Gardner, Jr., in *Roadside Food: Good Home-Style Cooking Across America*

3 pounds ground beef sirloin

½ cup mesquite-flavored barbecue sauce

2 cloves garlic, minced

1 tablespoon chili powder

½ teaspoon curry powder

½ teaspoon salt

½ teaspoon coarsely ground black pepper

1 cup grated Monterey Jack or extra-sharp cheddar cheese

½ small red onion, halved and thinly sliced

1. Mix all the ingredients except the cheese and onion together in a large mixing bowl until well combined. Shape into 6 patties, each 1 inch thick.
2. Lightly oil the grill or a skillet over medium-high heat and cook the burgers to the desired degree of doneness, at least 5 minutes per side for medium rare. Top with the cheese and onion for the last minute of cooking.

SERVE IT UP on toasted sesame seed buns or onion rolls

TOP IT OFF with lettuce and sliced tomato

KOREAN BULGOGI BURGERS

MAKES 4 BURGERS

Korean *bulgogi* gets our vote as one of the world's best barbecued meats. Thin slices of sirloin are marinated in a sweet soy sauce mixture and then grilled. The result is barbecued beef that is at once crisp and tender, sweet, salty, and spicy. We predict this burgerized version will become one of your favorites.

1 pound ground beef sirloin

¾ cup grated onion

1 tablespoon plus 1 teaspoon sugar

3 tablespoons soy sauce

½ teaspoon coarsely ground black pepper

1½ teaspoons toasted sesame oil

1 tablespoon plus 2 teaspoons dry sherry

2 cloves garlic, minced

1. In a medium-size mixing bowl, gently mix together the beef, ½ cup of the onion, 1 teaspoon of the sugar, 1 tablespoon of the soy sauce, the pepper, 1 teaspoon of the sesame oil, 1 tablespoon of the sherry, and half of the garlic. Form into 4 patties, each ¾ inch thick.
2. In a small bowl, mix together the remaining ¼ cup onion, 1 tablespoon sugar, 2 tablespoons soy sauce, ½ teaspoon sesame oil, 2 teaspoons sherry, and garlic. Set aside for topping.
3. Lightly oil the grill or a skillet over medium-high heat and cook the burgers to the desired degree of doneness, 3 to 5 minutes per side for medium rare.

SERVE IT UP on toasted and buttered hamburger or hoagie buns

TOP IT OFF with the onion–soy sauce mixture and slivered scallions (white and green parts)

PAMPAS BURGERS WITH CHIMICHURRI SAUCE

MAKES 4 BURGERS

Argentina produces some of the world's best beef, and that's the inspiration behind this simple grilled burger. It's paired with Chimichurri Sauce, a garlicky condiment commonly used as a meat and fish accompaniment throughout Latin America. We've added red bell peppers and olives to the sauce for a particularly Argentine accent.

1 pound ground beef sirloin

½ medium-size green bell pepper, seeded and finely diced

½ teaspoon salt

½ teaspoon coarsely ground black pepper

1. In a medium-size mixing bowl, gently mix together all the ingredients and form into 4 patties, each ½ inch thick.
2. Lightly oil the grill or a skillet over medium-high heat and cook the burgers to the desired degree of doneness, 5 to 6 minutes per side for medium rare.

SERVE IT UP on toasted sweet Cuban bread or French bread

TOP IT OFF with Chimichurri Sauce (recipe follows)

Chimichurri Sauce

MAKES 3/4 CUP

- 6 cloves garlic, peeled
- 1 bunch fresh flat-leaf parsley leaves
- ½ cup olive oil
- ¼ cup distilled white vinegar
- ¼ teaspoon coarsely ground black pepper
- ½ teaspoon red pepper flakes
- 1 teaspoon dried oregano
- ¼ cup chopped pitted black olives
- ½ medium-size red bell pepper, seeded and finely diced

Pulse the garlic and parsley together in a food processor until finely chopped. Add the oil, vinegar, black pepper, red pepper flakes, oregano, and olives and pulse until well combined but not smooth. Stir in the bell pepper. Taste and adjust the seasonings.

HOLY COW!

A 1,000-pound steer provides enough beef to make 1,000 quarter-pound burgers.

RICH MAN'S HAMBURGER

MAKES 1 BURGER

San Francisco chef and cookbook author Reed Hearon's restaurant, Rose Pistola, captured the culinary equivalent of an Oscar when it won the James Beard Foundation award for the Best New Restaurant in the country. We can attest to his formidable culinary talents. After taste-testing nearly a dozen burger recipes, Liz and her stomach were about to call it quits when she made Reed's burger—and wolfed down the entire half-pounder by herself! If that isn't the ultimate compliment to a great chef and a great burger, then we don't know what is. Reed suggests eating this at 2:00 A.M. with a 1996 claret. We say it's fabulous any time of day or night.

BURGER

½ pound lean beef top sirloin, cut into 1-inch chunks

1 shallot, minced

1 tablespoon minced fresh chives

1 tablespoon Dijon mustard

2 dashes Tabasco sauce

2 large egg yolks

2 dashes Worcestershire sauce

1 tablespoon cognac

½ teaspoon sea salt

4 teaspoons drained and chopped capers

1 tablespoon cracked black peppercorns, or to taste

1 tablespoon unsalted butter

MUSTARD HORSERADISH BUTTER

2 tablespoons unsalted butter

1 tablespoon peeled and grated fresh horseradish

2 tablespoons Dijon mustard

2 cloves garlic, minced

2 tablespoons chopped fresh flat-leaf parsley leaves

Grated zest of 1 lemon

Juice of ½ lemon

1 soft fresh roll or focaccia

1. To make the burger, pulse the beef in a food processor until it's coarsely ground. Gently stir in the shallot, chives, mustard, Tabasco, eggs, Worcestershire, cognac, sea salt, capers, and peppercorns. Form the mixture into a patty about 1½ inches thick.
2. Heat a small sauté pan over high heat until the pan is very hot. Melt the butter, then cook the burger to the desired degree of doneness. Reed prefers his crisp and brown on the outside but still raw and cool in the middle, which takes 2 to 3 minutes per side. Remove from the pan and set aside.
3. To make the mustard horseradish butter, combine all the ingredients in a food processor and process until smooth. Spread 1 tablespoon of the mixture on each side of the roll. Blot the pan you cooked the burger in with a paper towel. Fry the roll on both sides until warm and browned. Serve the burger open-faced.

TOP IT OFF with crumbled Roquefort or other good-quality blue cheese

BURGERS DIANE

MAKES 6 BURGERS

This flavorful burger was inspired by a classic Julia Child recipe for steak Diane. The thick, pungent sauce, with its bite of green peppercorns and zip of Worcestershire sauce, adds a touch of sophistication that will please the epicure in you.

> *"It is the Americans who have managed to crown minced beef as hamburger, and to send it round the world so that even the fussy French have taken to le boeuf haché, le hambourgaire."*
>
> Julia Child

1 tablespoon cornstarch
1 tablespoon Dijon mustard
1 cup beef broth
2 pounds ground beef sirloin
3 tablespoons green peppercorns packed in water, drained
¼ teaspoon soy sauce
1 tablespoon olive oil
¼ cup minced shallots
¼ cup chopped fresh flat-leaf parsley leaves
¼ teaspoon Worcestershire sauce
Juice of ½ lemon
1 teaspoon port or Madeira

1. In a small mixing bowl, combine the cornstarch, mustard, and broth and set aside.
2. Form the ground sirloin into 6 patties, each 1 inch thick, and set aside.
3. Place the peppercorns on a shallow plate and crush with the back of a spoon. Mix in the soy sauce and 1 teaspoon of the olive oil.
4. Press both sides of each burger into the peppercorn mixture, so the burgers are evenly studded and you have used up all the peppercorns.

5. Heat 1 teaspoon of the olive oil in a skillet over high heat and sear 3 of the burgers on both sides, 1 to 2 minutes per side. Remove from the pan and set aside. Repeat with the remaining 3 burgers.
6. Reduce the heat to medium, add the shallots and parsley, and stir to combine. Add the cornstarch mixture, Worcestershire, lemon juice, and port and cook, stirring, for 1 minute.
7. Carefully pour half the sauce into a second skillet. Place 3 burgers in each skillet, reduce the heat to medium-low, and cook, bathing the burgers in the simmering sauce by turning them over, for 3 to 5 minutes.

SERVE IT UP on toasted brioche buns

TOP IT OFF with some of the pan sauce and a pinch of chopped fresh flat-leaf parsley

MUSTARD PUTS DIJON ON THE MAP

In 1856, a clever man in Dijon, France, decided to use verjuice (the juice of unripened grapes) instead of vinegar in mustard. The result was a milder mustard, and Dijon eventually became known as the mustard capital of the world.

THE BIG MOCK WITH OUR OWN SPECIAL SAUCE

MAKES 1 BURGER

They say imitation is the sincerest form of flattery. So with our compliments to McDonald's, here's our copycat version of its most popular burger. You're probably wondering, *Why make my own when I can just hop in the car and cruise up to the drive-through?* Well, besides impressing the hell out of your friends, you can also sink your teeth into juicier, beefier patties and control exactly what goes into your double-decker burger.

- 6 ounces ground beef chuck
- 1 tablespoon grated onion
- ½ teaspoon salt
- ¼ teaspoon coarsely ground black pepper
- 1 tablespoon Our Own Special Sauce (page 30), or more to taste
- 2 hamburger bottom buns, toasted
- ¼ cup finely chopped lettuce, or more to taste
- 2 tablespoons chopped onion, or more to taste
- 2 slices American cheese
- 4 slices bread-and-butter pickles, or to taste
- 1 sesame seed top bun, toasted

1. In a small mixing bowl, gently combine the beef, grated onion, salt, and pepper. Divide the mixture in half and form into 2 patties, each ¼ inch thick.
2. Lightly oil a medium-size skillet over medium-high heat and cook the burgers to the desired degree of doneness, 2 to 4 minutes per side for medium. Remove from the heat.

3. Assemble the burger: Spread half the special sauce over one of the bottom buns, sprinkle a third of the lettuce and chopped onion on the bun, and top with 1 slice of cheese. Place one of the hamburger patties on top, then the other bottom bun. Slather on the remaining special sauce, sprinkle with half the remaining lettuce and onion, and top with 2 of the pickle slices. Top with the other hamburger patty and the remaining cheese, lettuce, onion, and pickles. Cap the sandwich with the toasted top bun.

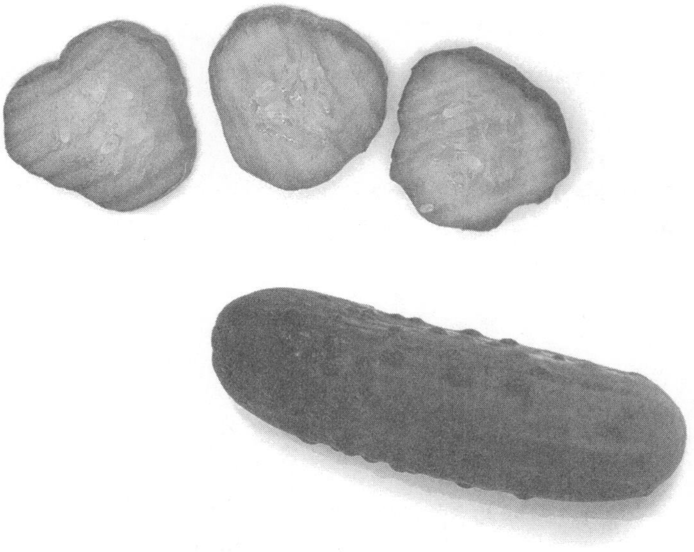

Our Own Special Sauce

MAKES 1/4 CUP

2 tablespoons Thousand Island dressing

1 tablespoon French dressing

1 tablespoon mayonnaise

1 tablespoon sweet pickle relish

1 teaspoon finely grated onion

½ teaspoon sugar

½ teaspoon distilled white vinegar

Pinch of salt

Combine all the ingredients in a small bowl and mix well. Refrigerate for at least 30 minutes to let the flavors develop.

McDONALD'S MISCELLANY

- **The first McDonald's, in Des Plaines, Illinois, is now a museum.**
- **McDonald's has more than 30,000 outlets in 121 countries.**
- **It has sold 12 hamburgers for every person in the world.**
- **The New Delhi McDonald's makes its burgers with mutton, since Hindus don't eat beef. Its Maharaja Mac is made with 2 mutton patties.**
- **According to an article in *Nation's Restaurant News*, 1 out of every 15 people got his or her first job at McDonald's.**

BARBECUED ROPA VIEJA BURGERS WITH ESCABECHE SPICE RUB THAT CURES

MAKES 6 BURGERS

Miami chef and cookbook author Norman Van Aken is famous for his innovative New World cuisine—an original blend of Latin, Caribbean, Asian, and American flavors. Norman has generously shared this recipe, which also appears in his book *Norman's New World Cuisine. Ropa vieja* (pronounced ROE-pa vee-A-ha), by the way, means "old clothes" in Spanish. If only old clothes looked as good as this tastes!

4 to 5 pounds chuck or flank steak

4 teaspoons Escabeche Spice Rub That Cures (page 33)

2 tablespoons annatto oil or olive oil

2 tablespoons unsalted butter

2 large onions, thinly sliced

12 cloves garlic, sliced

1 cup water

1 cup tomato sauce

3 tablespoons firmly packed light brown sugar

1 teaspoon dry mustard

½ cup fresh lemon juice

½ cup sherry wine vinegar

½ cup ketchup

2 tablespoons Worcestershire sauce

1 tablespoon freshly toasted and ground cumin seeds

1 tablespoon coarsely ground black pepper

1. Place the steak on a work surface and rub the spice rub evenly on each side. Heat the oil in a large, heavy saucepan or Dutch oven over medium-high heat and sear the meat on all sides. Remove from the pan and set aside. Add the butter to the pan. When it begins to foam, add the onions and garlic. Coat thoroughly with the butter and cook, stirring, until they are caramelized, about 15 minutes. Add ½ cup of the water and deglaze the pan, scraping up any browned bits from the bottom. Reduce the heat to very low and add the beef, tomato sauce, and remaining ½ cup water. Move the meat around and press down so that the liquid and some of the onions cover the meat. Cover the pan and let simmer for 2 hours, turning the meat after 1 hour.
2. Meanwhile, mix together the brown sugar, mustard, lemon juice, vinegar, ketchup, and Worcestershire in a small bowl. When the meat is done, uncover the pan, skim off any excess fat, and add the brown sugar mixture. Cover the pan and cook for 1 hour more.
3. Remove the meat from the pan and let cool. Reduce the sauce over high heat until thickened, 10 to 20 minutes. Shred the meat, discarding any bones and fat. Reduce the heat to low and return the shredded beef to the pan. Add the cumin and pepper and cook for 10 minutes.

SERVE IT UP on hamburger buns or wrapped in warm corn or flour tortillas

TOP IT OFF with a poached or fried egg

Escabeche Spice Rub That Cures

MAKES 1½ TABLESPOONS

1 ½ teaspoons cumin seeds

1 ½ teaspoons black peppercorns

¾ teaspoon sugar

¾ teaspoon salt

1. Place the cumin and peppercorns in a dry skillet over medium heat and toast, shaking the pan, until fragrant and slightly smoking, 30 to 60 seconds.
2. Transfer the mix to a spice grinder and pulverize until not quite finely ground. Place in a small bowl, add the sugar and salt, and mix.

EARLY MORNING BURGERS

Robert's has been open for business since 1926. Starting at 6:00 A.M., diners can grab a seat at the 14-stool counter for a mouthwatering onion-fried burger. The burger secret? Owner Edward Graham adds onions to the patties before grilling them.

Robert's Grill • 300 South Bickford Avenue • El Reno, OK 73036 • (405) 262-1262

JONATHAN WAXMAN'S HAMBURGERS

MAKES 8 BURGERS

Renowned chef Jonathan Waxman was the first to introduce California cuisine to New York with Jams, his iconic restaurant that made him a superstar in the 1980s. His latest restaurant, Washington Park, has opened to great acclaim, and diners are flocking to this Greenwich Village establishment. You'll want to eat there, too, after chowing down on this burger.

2 pounds top-end beef chuck, cut into 1-inch chunks

2 shallots, minced

2 cloves garlic, minced

1 teaspoon Worcestershire sauce

2 teaspoons whole-grain Dijon mustard

1 tablespoon fino sherry (preferably La Ina)

1 tablespoon extra virgin olive oil

1 teaspoon chopped fresh flat-leaf parsley leaves

1 teaspoon sea salt, plus more for the burgers, if desired

1 tablespoon soy sauce

1. On a large cutting board, use a 12-inch chef's knife to chop the meat until it is roughly minced. Place in a large mixing bowl. Add the shallots and garlic, but do not mix them in. Add all the remaining ingredients and, with a large wooden spoon, mix just until everything is incorporated. Form into 8 patties, each about ¾ inch thick.
2. Heat a large cast-iron skillet over medium-high heat. Just before cooking, lightly salt the tops and bottoms of the burgers, if you wish. Cook to the desired degree of doneness, 3 to 5 minutes per side for medium rare.

SERVE IT UP on kaiser rolls

JERRY'S BEST BEEF BURGERS

MAKES 6 BURGERS

Jane's husband, Jerry, created this Provence-inspired recipe, which soon became a family favorite. The seasonings give these burgers a wonderful aroma and a nice kick. We like them served with a generous dollop of prepared horseradish.

2 pounds ground beef sirloin

¼ cup minced shallots

3 tablespoons whole-grain Dijon mustard

3 tablespoons chopped fresh rosemary leaves

1½ teaspoons coarsely ground black pepper

¼ teaspoon salt

1. Blend all the ingredients together in a large mixing bowl, making sure your hands spread the seasoning evenly through the meat. Shape into 6 patties, each 1 inch thick.
2. Lightly oil the grill or a skillet over medium-high heat and cook the burgers to the desired degree of doneness, 6 to 8 minutes per side for medium.

SERVE IT UP on toasted sesame seed buns

TOP IT OFF with prepared horseradish, romaine lettuce, and sliced tomato or Tomato and Leek Salad (page 143)

SLOPPY JOE BURGERS

MAKES 8 GENEROUS SERVINGS

Sweet and tangy, this campfire favorite features a loose filling—a burger without boundaries. The sloppy joe has murky beginnings. Some think it was invented in the 1930s at a tavern in Sioux City, Iowa. We don't know about that, but we can tell you that the filling is also delicious with pasta or spooned over baked potatoes or rice.

2 tablespoons olive oil

1 large onion, finely chopped

1 large carrot, minced

1 celery stalk, minced

6 cloves garlic, minced

½ cup tomato paste

2½ cups tomato puree

3 tablespoons cider vinegar

¼ cup molasses

3 tablespoons Worcestershire sauce

2 pounds ground beef round

1. Heat a large skillet over medium heat. Add the olive oil, then the onion, carrot, celery, and garlic, and cook, stirring, until softened, 5 to 7 minutes. Stir in the tomato paste, tomato puree, vinegar, molasses, and Worcestershire and bring to a simmer. Reduce the heat to low and let simmer gently until thickened and the flavors have melded, 45 to 60 minutes. Add a little water to the sauce if it gets too thick or dry.

2. In another large skillet over medium-high heat, brown the ground beef until no longer pink, breaking it apart into small pieces. Drain the excess fat from the skillet. Add the sauce and simmer over medium-low heat until the flavors blend, at least 10 minutes.

SERVE IT UP by spooning ½ cup of the sloppy joe filling over half a toasted hamburger bun and topping with the other half

A CROSS SECTION OF NASHVILLE

We read that Rotier's attracts Nashville burger lovers from all walks of life: children, blue-haired ladies, couples out on dates. The burgers better be good for you to take your date to a burger joint filled with kids and seniors! At Rotier's, the burgers are piled high with all the fixings and skewered with a huge toothpick to keep them together.

Rotier's • 2413 Elliston Place • Nashville, TN 37203 • (615) 327-9892

CUBAN FRITA BURGERS

MAKES 8 BURGERS, OR 4 SERVINGS

These delicious little burgers always make Liz homesick for Miami, where she grew up. *Fritas* were very popular in Cuba, where they were sold at roadside stands. In Miami, there are places that still sell them like that. If you are ever there, you must try the *fritas* at El Rey de las Fritas in Little Havana. *¡Ay, qué rico!*

½ cup plain dry bread crumbs

¼ cup milk

1 pound ground beef round

1 small onion, finely chopped

1 large egg

2 cloves garlic, minced

2 teaspoons ketchup

1 teaspoon sweet paprika

1 teaspoon salt

½ teaspoon coarsely ground black pepper

½ teaspoon ground cumin

½ teaspoon dried oregano

1. Combine the bread crumbs and milk in a small mixing bowl and set aside.
2. Gently mix the beef, half of the onion, the egg, garlic, ketchup, paprika, salt, pepper, cumin, and oregano together in a medium-size mixing bowl. Fold in the bread crumb mixture and mix thoroughly. Form into 8 patties, each a little less than ½ inch thick.

3. Lightly oil the grill or a skillet over medium-high heat and cook the burgers to the desired degree of doneness, 2 to 4 minutes per side for medium.

SERVE IT UP on dinner rolls (each person gets 2 rolls)

TOP IT OFF with potato sticks (yes, the kind you buy in cans) and the remaining chopped onion

TACO BURGERS

MAKES 4 BURGERS

This is the favorite of Liz's big meat-eater husband, Ravi. He says it reminds him of the best meal he ever had at Taco Bell (he loves that place, so this is his highest compliment). You'll love the intense seasoning and how easy it is to make.

1 pound ground beef sirloin

¼ cup finely chopped onion

2 tablespoons taco seasoning

1 tablespoon tomato paste

1 tablespoon minced hot peppers (from a jar)

1. Gently mix together the beef, onion, taco seasoning, tomato paste, and hot peppers. Form into 4 patties, each ¾ inch thick.
2. Lightly oil the grill or a skillet over medium-high heat and cook the burgers to the desired degree of doneness, 3 to 5 minutes per side for medium.

SERVE IT UP on hamburger buns

TOP IT OFF with shredded extra-sharp cheddar cheese, shredded lettuce, and salsa

SCHOOL LUNCH ALL-STARS

The five favorite U.S. school lunches nationwide, according to the American School Food Service Association, are pizza, chicken nuggets, tacos, burritos, and hamburgers.

PIZZA BURGERS

MAKES 4 BURGERS

This burger was inspired by Liz's brother-in-law, Din. In his single days, he'd come home after a night out with the boys and fix an impromptu pizza on an English muffin. But inevitably, he'd fall asleep on the couch, while the muffin burned to a crisp in the oven. Din may not be able to cook to save his life, but he knows a good burger when he sees one.

1 pound ground beef round

1 cup marinara or pizza sauce

¼ cup finely chopped onion

2 cloves garlic, minced

½ teaspoon salt

¼ teaspoon coarsely ground black pepper

4 ounces mozzarella cheese, shredded

1. Gently mix together the beef, ½ cup of the marinara sauce, the onion, garlic, salt, and pepper. Divide the mixture into 8 patties, each just less than ½ inch thick.
2. Sprinkle half of the patties with the mozzarella cheese. Top each with a remaining patty and carefully seal the edges together.
3. Lightly oil the grill or a skillet over medium-high heat and cook the burgers to the desired degree of doneness, at least 4 to 5 minutes per side for medium. It's okay if some of the cheese oozes out.

SERVE IT UP on toasted English muffins

TOP IT OFF with pepperoni slices and the remaining ½ cup marinara sauce

TEXAS-STYLE BEEF BURGERS WITH PINTO BEANS, BACON, AND GREEN CHILES (AKA KNIFE-AND-FORK BURGERS)

MAKES 4 BURGERS

Robert Del Grande is the chef/owner of Houston's Cafe Annie, an award-winning restaurant that *Gourmet* magazine calls one of the top 50 restaurants in the nation. Cafe Annie is a showcase for southwestern cuisine, and this burger recipe that Robert so generously contributed reflects his Texas-size sensibility—and tastes. He advises that a knife and fork may be required if you really load up the burgers. Make sure you have a Texas-size appetite to tackle this meat eater's dream.

1 cup dried pinto beans, rinsed and picked over

4 cups water, plus more if needed

2 cloves garlic, peeled

1 small yellow onion, chopped

2 plum tomatoes, cut into ¼-inch dice

2 medium-size fresh serrano chile peppers, seeded and minced

1 teaspoon kosher salt

¼ cup fresh cilantro leaves, coarsely chopped

2 large fresh poblano, Anaheim, or New Mexico green chile peppers

8 thick slices smoked bacon

2 pounds freshly ground beef chuck

2 tablespoons olive oil

½ teaspoon salt

½ teaspoon coarsely ground black pepper

1. Combine the beans and water in a medium-size saucepan. Slowly bring to a boil, then reduce the heat to medium-low and simmer for 30 minutes. Add the garlic, onion, tomatoes, serranos, and kosher salt and continue to simmer, stirring occasionally, until the beans are tender, about 1 hour. Add more water, if necessary. The beans should be thick and not too soupy. (The beans can be prepared 1 day ahead. Refrigerate and reheat when needed.) Keep warm and, just before serving, bring to a simmer and stir in the cilantro.
2. Meanwhile, lightly rub the poblanos with oil, then char them over an open gas flame or under a hot broiler. Allow the chiles to cool. Scrape off the charred skins and discard the stems and seeds. Cut each chile lengthwise into ¼-inch-wide strips and set aside for topping.
3. In a large, heavy skillet over medium heat, cook the bacon, turning it occasionally, until crisp, 5 to 7 minutes. Transfer to paper towels to drain, then break into pieces and set aside for topping.
4. In a large mixing bowl, combine the ground chuck, olive oil, salt, and pepper. Shape the mixture into 4 patties, each 1 inch thick. Heat the grill or a skillet over medium-high heat and cook the burgers to the desired degree of doneness, 3 to 5 minutes per side for medium.

SERVE IT UP on toasted hamburger buns

TOP IT OFF with the bacon pieces, poblanos, and hot beans, along with grated sharp cheddar cheese

OH, CANADA

Pizza now ranks as the top fast food in America, but it's only number 4 in Canada, where hamburgers hold the top spot.

SALISBURY STEAK BURGERS

MAKES 4 BURGERS

Believe it or not, Dr. Atkins isn't the most famous physician to push a protein-rich diet. Back in 1888, Dr. James Henry Salisbury proclaimed that people should eat more protein and less starch. His recipe for good health? Chopped meat—with a dash of horseradish, mustard, or Worcestershire sauce. So enjoy this in good health!

1 pound ground beef sirloin
½ cup plain dry bread crumbs
1 medium-size onion, finely chopped
2 cloves garlic, minced
1 large egg
1 teaspoon salt
½ teaspoon coarsely ground black pepper
1 tablespoon canola oil
3 tablespoons cornstarch
2 cups beef broth
8 ounces white mushrooms, sliced
¼ cup ketchup
2 tablespoons Worcestershire sauce
½ teaspoon dry mustard

1. In a medium-size mixing bowl, gently mix together the beef, bread crumbs, half of the onion, the garlic, egg, salt, and pepper. Form into 4 patties, each ¾ inch thick.
2. Heat the oil in a large skillet over medium-high heat. Sauté the burgers until just cooked through, 3 to 5 minutes per side. Remove from the pan and set aside. Reserve the pan drippings.

3. In a small bowl, mix the cornstarch with 1 cup of the beef broth to make a slurry.
4. To the reserved drippings in the pan, add the remaining onion and the mushrooms and cook, stirring, over medium-high heat until just softened, about 2 minutes, scraping the browned bits off the bottom of the pan. Add the remaining 1 cup broth, the ketchup, Worcestershire, and mustard. Whisk in the slurry and bring to a boil for 1 minute. Reduce the heat to low, return the burgers to the pan, and simmer for 3 to 5 minutes.

SERVE IT UP on hamburger buns

TOP IT OFF with some of the pan sauce

HAMBURG'S FIRST COOKBOOK APPEARANCE

The first cookbook in America that included a recipe for Hamburg steak was Fannie Farmer's *1896 Boston Cooking-School Cookbook*.

M. F. K. FISHER–INSPIRED BURGERS

MAKES 4 BURGERS

Mary Frances Kennedy Fisher was one of America's most celebrated food writers. Her witty prose and vivid descriptions were food writing at its best—the perfect balance between the art of eating and the art of language. In her book *An Alphabet for Gourmets*, Fisher includes a recipe for hamburgers. This is our version of her recipe.

1½ pounds ground beef sirloin

1 cup good-quality red wine (please don't use cooking wine)

2 tablespoons unsalted butter

½ medium-size onion, finely chopped

½ cup finely chopped baby bok choy or broccoli stems

2 tablespoons minced fresh flat-leaf parsley leaves

2 tablespoons chopped scallions (white and green parts)

¼ cup Chinese oyster sauce

1. Shape the meat into 4 patties, each 1½ inches thick.
2. Heat a large cast-iron skillet over very high heat until smoking, then sear the burgers to the desired degree of doneness, 3 to 4 minutes per side for medium rare. Remove the burgers from the skillet and set aside.
3. Remove the skillet from the heat and swirl in the wine and butter. Return the skillet to medium-high heat and add the onion, bok choy, parsley, and scallions. Cover the skillet and bring the mixture to a boil. Remove from the heat and stir in the oyster sauce.

SERVE IT UP on toasted sesame seed buns

TOP IT OFF with some of the pan sauce

GUINNESS PUB BURGERS

MAKES 4 BURGERS

This is for the stouthearted, so to speak. If you like the strong, malty, yeasty flavor that makes Guinness so famous, you'll love this burger. In the 1920s, the beer's advertising slogan was "Guinness is good for you." In fact, hospitals in England used to dispense Guinness to patients. (This is, of course, no longer true.)

1 pound ground beef round

¼ cup Guinness Draught beer

2 teaspoons dry mustard

½ teaspoon ground ginger

2 cloves garlic, minced

1 teaspoon salt

½ teaspoon coarsely ground black pepper

2 tablespoons unsalted butter

¼ cup minced scallions (white and green parts)

1. In a medium-size mixing bowl, gently mix together the beef, beer, mustard, ginger, garlic, salt, and pepper. Form the mixture into 4 patties, each ¾ inch thick.
2. Melt the butter in a large skillet over medium-high heat and cook the burgers to the desired degree of doneness, 3 to 5 minutes per side for medium. Remove from the skillet. Add the scallions to the skillet and cook, stirring, until just wilted, 1 to 2 minutes.

SERVE IT UP on toasted sesame seed buns

TOP IT OFF with some of the pan sauce

MARK PEEL'S GORGONZOLA HAMBURGERS ON NANCY SILVERTON'S HAMBURGER BUNS

MAKES 4 BURGERS

Mark Peel and his pastry chef wife, Nancy Silverton, treat diners at their Los Angeles restaurant, Campanile, and the La Brea Bakery to the sublime flavors of California-Mediterranean cuisine. Those flavors are reflected in this hearty and pungent burger.

1½ pounds ground beef chuck

1 teaspoon kosher salt

1 teaspoon coarsely ground black pepper

3 ounces Gorgonzola cheese

1 tablespoon vegetable oil, if pan-frying

1. Combine the ground chuck, salt, and pepper in a medium-size mixing bowl and mix gently but thoroughly to combine. Divide the meat into 4 equal portions. Form each portion into a ball and poke your finger into the center to make a small cavity. Put about 1 teaspoon of the Gorgonzola in each cavity, then pinch it closed. Gently flatten each ball into a patty about 1 inch thick.
2. Heat the grill or a skillet over medium-high heat. If pan-frying, heat the oil in the pan. Cook the burgers to the desired degree of doneness, about 7 minutes per side for medium.

SERVE IT UP on grilled or toasted Nancy Silverton's Hamburger Buns (recipe follows)

TOP IT OFF with Dijon mustard or ketchup, sliced tomato, onion, and iceberg lettuce

Nancy Silverton's Hamburger Buns

MAKES 12 BUNS

These are smaller, denser, and sweeter than your standard supermarket buns. They require time but are worth it. The buns will keep in the freezer for up to two months.

1 cup plus 2 tablespoons whole milk

1 tablespoon active dry yeast or 1 tablespoon plus 1 teaspoon (1 ounce) packed fresh yeast

¼ cup sugar

3¾ cups plus 2 tablespoons unbleached all-purpose flour

2 extra-large eggs, lightly beaten

1 tablespoon kosher salt

3 tablespoons unsalted butter, softened but not greasy

Vegetable oil, for coating the bowl

1. In a small saucepan over medium heat, warm the milk until it's just warm to the touch. Place the milk, yeast, sugar, and flour in the bowl of an electric mixer fitted with the dough hook and mix on low speed until the ingredients are combined, about 2 minutes.
2. Measure out ⅓ cup of the eggs and discard the rest. Add the eggs and salt to the bowl and mix on high speed until the dough is smooth and shiny, 4 to 5 minutes. Turn the mixer down to medium speed, add the butter in small pieces, turn the mixer up to high speed, and mix for 1 minute, until the butter is incorporated.
3. Turn the dough out onto a lightly floured work surface and knead it a few times to gather it into a ball. Clean the mixing bowl and lightly coat it with vegetable oil. Return the dough to the oiled bowl, cover tightly with plastic wrap, and set aside in a warm place until the dough has doubled in size, 1 to 1½ hours.
4. Turn the dough out onto a floured work surface and cut into 12 equal-size pieces with a dough cutter. Tuck under the edges of each piece, cover the pieces with a clean cloth, and let rest for 15 minutes.

5. Working with one piece at a time and keeping the rest covered with the cloth, shape the dough into a ball by cupping your hand lightly around it and rounding it against the work surface to form a smooth bun. Begin slowly and increase the speed as the ball becomes tighter and smoother. Use as little flour as possible to prevent sticking. If there is not enough friction between the work surface and the dough, spritz the work surface lightly with water from a spray bottle. As each bun is shaped, check to be sure it is smooth and taut and the surface of the dough is not torn.
6. Place the buns at least 2 inches apart, smooth side up, on parchment paper–lined baking sheets. Press down gently on each bun to flatten it into a disk. Place each baking sheet in a large plastic garbage bag and blow air into the bag, creating a dome of air that will allow room for the dough to rise. Set aside in a warm place to rise until spongy to the touch, 45 to 60 minutes.
7. Preheat the oven to 500°F. Just before baking, place a few cups of ice in a baking dish and place the dish in the oven. Close the door to create steam. Reduce the oven temperature to 450°F and bake the buns until they're a deep golden brown, 15 to 20 minutes. Let sit for 5 minutes before splitting and toasting. Once completely cooled, these buns freeze nicely.

HAMBURG MAKES IT ONTO DELMONICO'S MENU

New York's Delmonico's restaurant had America's first printed menu in 1836, which listed Hamburg steak as one of its most expensive items, at 10 cents. Hamburg steak was a piece of beef that was pounded and tenderized, not a ground meat patty.

LATE-NIGHT BEEF BURGER WITH CHEDDAR, HORSERADISH, AND ONION

MAKES 1 BURGER*

Baseball's loss has been the food world's gain. In 1985, Michael Schlow traded a baseball scholarship for a chef's toque and hasn't looked back since. He doesn't have time to, because he's too busy winning accolades: *Food & Wine* magazine called him one of the Top Ten New Chefs in the Country and named his Boston restaurant, Radius, the Best New Restaurant in 2000. Michael confesses that this burger is "nice and messy, and it makes me quite happy around midnight."

- 1 tablespoon unsalted butter
- ½ small red onion, thinly sliced
- ½ pound ground beef (20 percent fat)
- 1 tablespoon extra virgin olive oil
- Kosher salt and coarsely ground black pepper to taste
- 1 tablespoon prepared horseradish
- 3 tablespoons mayonnaise
- 1 thick slice extra-sharp cheddar cheese (2 ounces), for topping

1. In a small skillet, melt the butter over medium heat. Add the onion, reduce the heat to medium-low, and cook until very soft and caramelized, 12 to 14 minutes, stirring occasionally. Remove from the heat and set aside for topping.
2. In a small mixing bowl, mix the ground beef with the olive oil and salt and pepper. Form the seasoned meat into a large, slightly flattened patty about 1½ inches thick and refrigerate for 10 minutes.
3. In a small bowl, combine the horseradish, mayonnaise, and a pinch of pepper. Set aside for topping.

*OR, ACCORDING TO MICHAEL, MAKES 1 VERY LARGE LATE-NIGHT STOMACHACHE (BUT IT TASTES REALLY GOOD)

4. Heat a medium-size skillet over medium-high heat until hot. Cook the burger to the desired degree of doneness (Schlow likes medium rare, which is 2 to 4 minutes per side for a burger this size). Remove from the skillet and let rest for 2 to 3 minutes.

SERVE IT UP on an extra-large English muffin, sliced and toasted with the cheese on the top half

TOP IT OFF with the caramelized onions and horseradish mayonnaise

MYSTERIOUS ORIGINS

Who invented the cheeseburger? Who knows. But here are some who lay claim to it.

1924 **Lionel Sternberger at the Rite Spot Restaurant in Pasadena, California, supposedly topped a ground beef patty with cheese and called it a "cheese hamburger."**

1934 **In Louisville, Kentucky, Margaret and Carl Kaelin charged 15 cents for their restaurant's special Kaelin's Cheeseburger.**

1935 **Louis E. Ballast created his cheeseburger at the Humpty Dumpty Barrel Drive-In in Denver, Colorado. Ballast tried to trademark the word *cheeseburger* but was unsuccessful.**

BULGARIAN BURGERS

MAKES 4 BURGERS

Steven Raichlen, author of *The Barbecue! Bible* and numerous other cookbooks, is the undisputed king of barbecue. Steven is so passionate about it that he even teaches a "Barbecue University" course in West Virginia. Steven says that Bulgarian burgers, which appear in *The Barbecue! Bible*, are one of his favorites. They're one of ours, too.

8 ounces ground veal

8 ounces ground pork

1 small onion, minced

3 tablespoons minced fresh flat-leaf parsley leaves

1 teaspoon salt, or more to taste

Generous ½ teaspoon ground cumin, or more to taste

½ teaspoon coarsely ground black pepper, or more to taste

1. Combine all the ingredients in a large mixing bowl and gently mix with a wooden spoon. Test the mixture for seasoning by sautéing a tiny portion in a nonstick skillet until cooked through. Taste and adjust the seasonings; the mixture should be highly seasoned.
2. Divide the meat into 4 equal portions. Lightly wet your hands with cold water, then form each portion into a patty about ¾ inch thick.
3. Lightly oil the grill or a skillet over high heat and cook the burgers to the desired degree of doneness, 4 to 5 minutes per side for medium.

SERVE IT UP on crusty rolls or country bread

TOP IT OFF with Eggplant Feta Salad (page 79)

MEAT LOAF BURGERS
WITH TANGY TOMATO SAUCE

MAKES 6 BURGERS

These comfort burgers have all the mouthwatering goodness of meat loaf—only we took the bread out of the meat loaf mix and put it on the outside so you can hold the whole thing in your hands. The secret to this tasty burger is the mixture of beef and pork.

1 pound ground beef round

¾ pound ground pork

One 6-ounce can tomato paste

1 teaspoon salt

1 teaspoon coarsely ground black pepper

3 cloves garlic, minced

1 small onion, chopped

2 teaspoons chopped fresh oregano leaves or 1 teaspoon dried

1 teaspoon chopped fresh thyme leaves or ½ teaspoon dried

1. In a large mixing bowl, gently mix all the ingredients together. Form into 6 patties, each 1 inch thick.
2. Lightly oil the grill or a skillet over medium-high heat and cook the burgers to the desired degree of doneness, 6 to 8 minutes per side for medium.

SERVE IT UP on toasted white bread or thick-sliced country bread

TOP IT OFF with Tangy Tomato Sauce (recipe follows) or Kick-Ass Ketchup (page 17)

Tangy Tomato Sauce

MAKES 1 CUP

¼ cup tomato sauce

¼ cup cider vinegar

¼ cup firmly packed light brown sugar

¼ cup Dijon mustard

Mix together all the ingredients in a small bowl.

THE EARL'S DEAL

Eighteenth-century British politician John Montagu, the fourth earl of Sandwich, is credited with naming the sandwich. Apparently, he took to eating beef between slices of toast so that he could continue to play cards uninterrupted.

SWEDISH MEATBALL BURGERS

MAKES 6 BURGERS

This classic cocktail favorite is usually served in tiny meatball portions. But as a main course, Swedish meatballs are traditionally served with mashed potatoes and lingonberry sauce. In our rendition, the meatball grows in size and is served in its own pan sauce.

¾ pound ground pork

½ pound ground beef round

½ cup plain dry bread crumbs

1 medium-size onion, finely chopped

¼ cup milk

1 large egg

½ teaspoon ground nutmeg

¾ teaspoon ground allspice

1 ¼ teaspoons salt

¾ teaspoon coarsely ground black pepper

1 tablespoon canola oil

2 tablespoons cornstarch

1 ½ cups beef broth

3 tablespoons dry sherry

2 teaspoons Worcestershire sauce

2 tablespoons sour cream

2 tablespoons chopped fresh dill

1. Gently mix together the pork, beef, bread crumbs, half of the onion, the milk, egg, nutmeg, ½ teaspoon of the allspice, 1 teaspoon of the salt, and ½ teaspoon of the pepper. Form the mixture into 6 patties, each ¾ inch thick.
2. Heat the oil in a large skillet over medium-high heat. Add the burgers and sauté until just cooked through, 3 to 5 minutes per side. Remove from the pan and set aside. Reserve the drippings in the pan.
3. In a small bowl, whisk together the cornstarch and ¾ cup of the beef broth. Set aside.
4. To the reserved drippings in the pan, add the remaining onion and the sherry. Cook over medium-high heat, scraping the browned bits off the bottom of the pan. Add the remaining ¾ cup broth, bring to a boil, stir in the cornstarch mixture, and bring to a boil again for 1 minute. Return the burgers to the pan and simmer for 2 to 4 minutes.
5. Remove the skillet from the heat and stir in the remaining ¼ teaspoon allspice, ¼ teaspoon salt, and ¼ teaspoon pepper, along with the Worcestershire, sour cream, and dill.

SERVE IT UP on hard rolls or rye bread

TOP IT OFF with some of the pan sauce

ENGLISH USAGE

In England, a "bap" is a hamburger bun.

GRILLED MAPLE MUSTARD PORK BURGERS

MAKES 4 BURGERS

Call this the quintessential North American burger, since maple trees are found only in North America. Its honeyed richness makes this burger great cooked in a grill pan but spectacular when barbecued.

1 pound fresh lightly seasoned pork sausage, casings removed

1 small onion, chopped

2 cloves garlic, minced

½ teaspoon salt

¼ teaspoon coarsely ground black pepper

3 tablespoons pure maple syrup

2 tablespoons Dijon mustard

1 tablespoon cider vinegar

½ teaspoon dry mustard

½ teaspoon grated orange zest

½ teaspoon curry powder

1. In a medium-size mixing bowl, mix together the sausage, onion, garlic, salt, and pepper until well combined. Shape into 4 patties, each ½ inch thick.
2. In a small bowl, whisk together the maple syrup, Dijon mustard, vinegar, dry mustard, orange zest, and curry powder. Reserve half of this mixture for topping.
3. Lightly oil the grill or a skillet over medium-high heat and cook the burgers for 5 minutes. Flip the burgers, baste with the maple syrup mixture, and cook until cooked through, about 5 minutes more.

SERVE IT UP on kaiser rolls or toasted egg bread or challah

TOP IT OFF with the remaining maple syrup mixture

MUSTARD IN THE MEDICINE CHEST?

Mustard stimulates blood circulation, which is why mustard plasters are used to increase blood flow to inflamed areas of the body. Some people believe that sprinkling mustard flour in your socks can ward off frostbite.

HONEY MUSTARD PORK BURGERS ON CHEDDAR THYME BISCUITS

MAKES 6 BURGERS

These hearty, sausage-flavored burgers are perfectly paired with soft, flaky biscuits—ideal for Sunday brunch. You could also use a mixture of pork and beef for a variation.

1 pound ground pork

¼ cup honey

2 tablespoons Dijon mustard

1 teaspoon salt

1 teaspoon coarsely ground black pepper

1½ teaspoons chopped fresh thyme leaves or ¾ teaspoon dried

¼ teaspoon ground nutmeg

1. In a medium-size mixing bowl, gently combine the pork, 2 tablespoons of the honey, 1 tablespoon of the mustard, the salt, pepper, thyme, and nutmeg. Form the mixture into 6 patties, each ½ inch thick.
2. In a small bowl, mix together the remaining 2 tablespoons honey and 1 tablespoon mustard. Set aside for topping.
3. Lightly oil the grill or a skillet over medium-high heat and cook the burgers to the desired degree of doneness, 4 to 6 minutes per side for medium.

SERVE IT UP on Cheddar Thyme Biscuits (recipe follows)

TOP IT OFF with the honey-mustard mixture

Cheddar Thyme Biscuits

MAKES 12 BISCUITS

This recipe makes 12 biscuits—twice the number of pork patties. But after tasting these fluffy biscuits, you'll be hard-pressed to find any complaints about leftovers.

2 cups plus 2 tablespoons all-purpose flour

2½ teaspoons sugar

2½ teaspoons baking powder

¾ teaspoon baking soda

1½ teaspoons salt

6 tablespoons (¾ stick) cold unsalted butter, cut into large dice

8 ounces extra-sharp cheddar cheese, grated

1½ tablespoons chopped fresh thyme leaves or 2 teaspoons dried

1 cup buttermilk

1. Preheat the oven to 450°F.
2. In a large mixing bowl, whisk together the flour, sugar, baking powder, baking soda, and salt. Cut in the butter with your fingers or a pastry blender until the mixture has the texture of coarse meal. Stir in the cheese and thyme. Pour in the buttermilk and stir until just combined.
3. Drop the dough in 12 portions onto a nonstick baking sheet. Bake until just golden, 14 to 16 minutes.

MUSTARD MAKER TO THE QUEEN

In 1886, Jeremiah Colman was appointed mustard maker to England's Queen Victoria after he created a way to make mustard powder that retained its spiciness. Colman's name lives on in the company he founded, Colman's Mustard.

CHOP SUEY BURGERS

MAKES 6 BURGERS

The origins of chop suey may be as mysterious as what goes in it. But we do know that nowhere in China will you find chop suey on the menu—such a dish just doesn't exist there. Food experts suspect it was purely a Chinese-American invention that goes back to the 1800s. Consider this version a Chinese-American sloppy joe.

1 pound ground pork

1 teaspoon soy sauce

2 tablespoons Chinese oyster sauce

1 medium-size yellow onion, chopped

1 tablespoon canola oil

1 cup chopped bok choy

¼ cup diced bamboo shoots

4 ounces white mushrooms, sliced

¼ cup sliced water chestnuts, drained

1 celery stalk, sliced

1 cup chicken broth

2 tablespoons cornstarch

¼ cup water

1. In a large nonstick skillet over medium-high heat, sauté the pork with the soy sauce, 1 tablespoon of the oyster sauce, and the onion until the meat is no longer pink, 3 to 5 minutes. Transfer to a medium-size mixing bowl and set aside. Wipe the skillet clean.
2. Place the skillet over high heat until it is smoking. Add the oil and swirl until it is very hot. Add the bok choy, bamboo shoots, mushrooms, water chestnuts, and celery and cook, stirring, until the vegetables

are just softened, 2 to 4 minutes. Return the pork to the skillet and add the chicken broth. Bring to a boil, then reduce the heat to medium-low and simmer for 10 minutes.

3. In a small bowl, mix together the remaining 1 tablespoon oyster sauce, the cornstarch, and water. Add this mixture to the skillet and bring to a boil for about 1 minute, until thickened.

SERVE IT UP on toasted French bread

TOP IT OFF with chopped scallions (white and green parts)

MADE IN CHINA

Ketchup, that all-American condiment, was actually invented by the Chinese. They called it *ke-tsiap* and made it with pickled fish and spices—but no tomatoes. It was some enterprising New Englanders who mixed tomatoes into the sauce, creating what we now know as ketchup.

NORTH CAROLINA CHOPPED BARBECUED PORK BURGERS

MAKES 6 TO 8 BURGERS

Norma Jean Darden is one of the biggest boosters of southern food in New York and the owner of two soul food restaurants, Miss Maude's Spoonbread Too and Miss Mamie's Spoonbread Too, and a catering company, Spoonbread Catering. She is also the coauthor of the memoir/cookbook *Spoonbread and Strawberry Wine*, based on family recipes from her southern childhood. She kindly shares her North Carolina–style burger with us, which is adapted from her cookbook.

2 tablespoons vegetable oil

One 2-pound pork shoulder roast

1 teaspoon salt

1 teaspoon celery seeds

⅛ teaspoon ground cinnamon

⅓ cup cider vinegar, plus more for seasoning

½ cup ketchup

½ teaspoon chili powder

½ teaspoon ground nutmeg

½ teaspoon sugar

1 cup water

1. Preheat the oven to 325°F. In a Dutch oven over medium-high heat, heat the oil, then brown the roast on all sides.
2. Mix the remaining ingredients together in a medium-size nonreactive saucepan and bring to a boil. Pour over the roast and cover. Bake until fork tender, about 40 minutes per pound, basting occasionally with the pan drippings.

3. Transfer the roast to a cutting board. Remove the meat from the bone and chop into fairly fine pieces.

SERVE IT UP sloppy joe style on toasted hamburger buns

TOP IT OFF with a splash of cider vinegar, hot sauce to taste, and coleslaw heaped on top

CHEESE WHIZ

We hear that an electric train runs around on the ceiling as diners chow down below. But it's cheese that takes center stage at Cheesy Jane's, with American, Swiss, Tillamook Cheddar, blue, pepper Jack, and provolone. Order the Plain Jane if you don't want the bun, or get a cheddar burger with the works—refried beans, Fritos, onions, and picante sauce.

Cheesy Jane's • 4200 Broadway • San Antonio, TX 78209 • (210) 826-0800

www.cheesyjanes.com

ANDOUILLE BAYOU BURGERS WITH RED PEPPER MAYO

MAKES 6 BURGERS

Smoky and spicy, these Cajun-inspired burgers are made for sausage fans. Andouille is a delicious smoked pork sausage used in Cajun specialties such as jambalaya and gumbo. If you can't get andouille, use any other spicy pork sausage instead.

½ pound andouille sausage meat, finely chopped (see Ingredient Sources, page 229)

2½ pounds ground beef chuck

1 medium-size green bell pepper, seeded and diced

½ small red onion, minced

1½ teaspoons salt

1½ teaspoons fennel seeds, crushed

Pinch of cayenne pepper

1. In a large mixing bowl, gently mix together all the ingredients. Shape into 6 patties, each 1 inch thick.
2. Lightly oil the grill or a skillet over medium-high heat and cook the burgers to the desired degree of doneness, 4 to 6 minutes per side for medium rare.

SERVE IT UP on focaccia or toasted sesame seed buns

TOP IT OFF with Red Pepper Mayo (recipe follows) and grilled onions or Fiesta Corn Salsa (page 103)

Red Pepper Mayo

MAKES ABOUT 3/4 CUP

One 3- to 4-ounce jar roasted red peppers, drained

½ cup mayonnaise

1 tablespoon minced shallots

1. Place all the ingredients in a food processor and process until smooth.
2. Set aside for at least 30 minutes to let the flavors develop.

OBJETS D'HAMBURGER

Daytona Beach, Florida, is home to the International Hamburger Hall of Fame. The Hamburger Museum boasts more than 1,000 hamburger-related objects, including biscuit jars, clocks, erasers, music boxes, salt and pepper shakers, and—get this—a waterbed, complete with a sesame seed bedspread and pillows. Harry Sperl, aka Hamburger Harry, is the museum's founder and collector of these burger novelties. He even has a hamburger Harley and a Big Boy doll clutching a hamburger.

TERIYAKI HAM BURGERS WITH GRILLED GINGER PINEAPPLE

MAKES 4 BURGERS

This burger is heavenly if you love to "pig" out. Studded with chunks of ham, these pork patties get a Hawaiian touch from the teriyaki sauce and grilled pineapple. After you taste them, we guarantee the oinks won't be coming from the pork.

1½ pounds ground pork

6 ounces baked Virginia ham, cut into ½-inch dice

1 tablespoon peeled and minced fresh ginger

2 cloves garlic, minced

1 tablespoon soy sauce

¾ cup teriyaki sauce

1. Gently combine all the ingredients except the teriyaki sauce in a large mixing bowl. Form into 4 patties, each 1 inch thick. Pour ¼ cup of the teriyaki sauce into a small bowl and brush all over the burgers.
2. Lightly oil the grill or a skillet over medium-high heat and cook the burgers until well done, 4 to 6 minutes per side, basting with the remaining teriyaki sauce once each side has browned.

SERVE IT UP on kaiser rolls

TOP IT OFF with Grilled Ginger Pineapple (recipe follows)

Grilled Ginger Pineapple

MAKES 4 SERVINGS

¾ cup firmly packed light brown sugar

1 teaspoon peeled and minced fresh ginger

1 teaspoon ground ginger

1 ripe pineapple, peeled, cored, and cut into ¾-inch-thick rings

½ cup (1 stick) unsalted butter, melted

1. In a small bowl, mix together the brown sugar, fresh ginger, and ground ginger.
2. Dip the pineapple rounds in the melted butter, then in the brown sugar mixture, coating them evenly.
3. Lightly oil the grill or a grill pan over medium-high heat and cook the pineapple until golden brown and softened, 4 to 7 minutes per side.

BURGERMANIA

According to *The Dictionary of American Food and Drink*, Americans eat 3 hamburgers per week per person. That's about 38 billion hamburgers annually, or 59 percent of all sandwiches consumed.

SPICY TOFU AND PORK BURGERS

MAKES 6 BURGERS

This may be the only burger in the book that is actually steamed. Don't wrinkle your nose! It's very tasty, thanks to the spicy chili garlic sauce, which will most certainly clear your sinuses, if you dare swallow a spoonful. We don't suggest it.

1 pound ground pork

2 teaspoons Asian chili garlic sauce

¾ teaspoon salt

½ teaspoon sugar

½ teaspoon cornstarch

One 12-ounce package firm tofu, drained

1 large egg, lightly beaten

¼ teaspoon ground white pepper

½ teaspoon toasted sesame oil

1 scallion (white and green parts), minced

1. In a large mixing bowl, combine the pork, chili garlic sauce, ¼ teaspoon of the salt, ¼ teaspoon of the sugar, and the cornstarch. Set aside.
2. Mash the tofu in a large bowl, then place it in a double thickness of cheesecloth or a clean kitchen towel. Twist the ends together and squeeze out as much water as possible. Repeat twice. Scoop the tofu out into a medium-size mixing bowl and add the remaining ½ teaspoon salt, ¼ teaspoon sugar, the egg, white pepper, sesame oil, and scallion. Mix well, then add to the pork mixture and mix again. Form into 6 patties, each 1 inch thick.

3. In a steamer, steam the burgers until cooked all the way through, 7 to 10 minutes. Remove from the steamer and serve immediately.

SERVE IT UP wrapped in warm flour tortillas or on Japanese rice patties (see page 126)

TOP IT OFF with a judicious sprinkling of chili garlic sauce

DIG THIS

Archaeologist wannabes can go on a real dinosaur dig with celebrated paleontologists in the Badlands of Montana. After a hard day's work excavating in the field, they gather for some hearty food, including the famous three-quarter-pound T-Rex Burger, which leader Vicki Clouse swears is "the best burger you've ever had."

Dino Dyna (camp's eating area)

Vicki Clouse and Tom "TC" Chestnut • Badlands of Montana

(800) 662-6132, ext. 3716, or (406) 265-3716

SEEKH KEBAB BURGERS

MAKES 4 BURGERS

These are jumbo versions of a popular Indian dish. They are usually shaped into little cigars and made with lamb, but you can use beef if you want. Garam masala is a very flavorful blend of spices that can be found in many Middle Eastern or Asian grocery stores. *Seekh kebab* is highly seasoned and great served with Cucumber Mint Sauce (page 81). Or try it cold with some ketchup on top.

1 pound ground lamb

¼ cup plain dry bread crumbs

1 large egg

2 cloves garlic, minced

1 tablespoon minced fresh cilantro leaves

1 teaspoon salt

½ teaspoon coarsely ground black pepper

1 teaspoon ground cumin

1 teaspoon sweet paprika

1 teaspoon ground coriander

¾ teaspoon ground ginger

½ teaspoon turmeric

½ teaspoon garam masala (optional)

2 tablespoons canola oil

1. In a medium-size mixing bowl, gently combine all the ingredients except the oil. Cover with plastic wrap and refrigerate for at least 30 minutes to let the flavors develop.
2. Form the mixture into 4 patties, each ½ inch thick.

3. Lightly oil the grill or heat the oil in a large nonstick skillet over medium-high heat. Add the burgers and cook until well browned, at least 5 to 7 minutes per side.

SERVE IT UP in warm pita pockets

TOP IT OFF with chopped onion and chopped fresh cilantro

FOG CITY GRILLED LAMB BURGERS WITH TOMATO MINT CHUTNEY AND ROASTED BELL PEPPER CHOW-CHOW

MAKES 4 BURGERS

Put the Fog City Diner on your "must see" list the next time you're in San Francisco. This former club car is now a dining landmark, not only for its unusual architecture but also for its retro yet modern menu. Diner classics such as burgers and meat loaf are served up alongside *moo shu* burritos and oysters on the half shell. Chef Trevor White invented this burger in Hawaii when he had more lamb than he knew what to do with. "We'd get entire lambs delivered to the restaurant, and I'd have to think of ways to use it all," he says. As they say, necessity is the mother of invention, and we think this is a damn good one.

2 pounds boneless lamb (shoulder or leg), ground twice

½ cup dried mushrooms, soaked in hot water to cover until soft, then drained, or 1 cup finely chopped fresh white mushrooms

1 tablespoon minced garlic

2 teaspoons minced fresh rosemary leaves

1 tablespoon salt

1 tablespoon coarsely ground black pepper

8 ounces fontina cheese, cut into 4 slices

1. In a large mixing bowl, mix together the lamb, mushrooms, garlic, rosemary, salt, and pepper. Form into 4 patties, each about 1½ inches thick.

2. Lightly oil the grill or a skillet over medium-high heat and cook the burgers to the desired degree of doneness, 5 to 7 minutes per side for medium. After flipping the burgers the first time, place a slice of cheese on top of each to melt while they finish cooking.

SERVE IT UP on lightly toasted rosemary focaccia

TOP IT OFF with the Tomato Mint Chutney and Roasted Bell Pepper Chow-Chow (recipes follow)

WHERE YOU AND YOUR CANINE CAN DINE

To call San Francisco's Fog City Diner a mere diner is like calling a Porsche just a car. This neon and steel restaurant boasts mahogany wood, polished brass, and leather booths. And it doesn't just cater to you; it'll treat your pooch as well—with water and biscuits when the weather's warm.

Fog City Diner • 1300 Battery Street • San Francisco, CA 94111 • (415) 982-2000

www.fogcitydiner.cc

Tomato Mint Chutney

MAKES 1 TO 1½ CUPS

This is Fog City's inventive spin on the more traditional mint jelly accompaniment for lamb.

1¼ pounds plum tomatoes, plunged into boiling water for 1 minute, peeled, and seeded

½ cup sugar

6 cloves garlic, minced

2 teaspoons cayenne pepper

¾ cup cider vinegar

2 tablespoons fresh mint leaves cut into thin ribbons

1 tablespoon salt

¼ cup golden raisins or black currants

Combine the tomatoes, sugar, garlic, cayenne, vinegar, mint, and salt in a medium-size, heavy-bottomed nonreactive saucepan. Bring to a boil, reduce the heat to low, and simmer, stirring occasionally, until thickened, 15 to 18 minutes. Add the raisins and let the sauce simmer for 10 minutes more. Remove from the heat and allow to cool. This will keep, tightly covered, in the refrigerator for up to 1 week.

Roasted Bell Pepper Chow-Chow

MAKES 1 TO 1½ CUPS

Chow-chow was originally a Chinese condiment made from orange peel and ginger. Now it means any mustard-flavored relish.

1 medium-size red bell pepper

1 medium-size green bell pepper

1 medium-size yellow bell pepper

½ cup minced shallots

2 tablespoons minced fresh rosemary leaves

1 cup red wine vinegar

⅔ cup sugar

1 tablespoon smoked paprika (regular is fine if you can't find smoked)

1 teaspoon yellow mustard seeds

1 teaspoon salt

1 teaspoon coarsely ground black pepper

1. Over an open flame or under the broiler, roast the bell peppers evenly on all sides until the skins are charred. Place them in a bowl and cover with plastic wrap until cool. Scrape off the skins and remove the ribs and seeds. Do not rinse with water; this will cause the flavor to go down the drain. Finely cut the peppers into matchsticks.
2. Place all the ingredients in a medium-size nonreactive saucepan over medium-high heat. Bring to a boil, reduce the heat to low, and simmer until thickened, 20 to 30 minutes. Remove from the heat and let cool. This will keep, tightly covered, in the refrigerator for up to 1 week.

HELLENIC LAMB BURGERS WITH EGGPLANT FETA SALAD

MAKES 4 BURGERS

Rich with thyme and oregano, this burger embodies classic Greek flavors. But it's the sweet-and-sour grilled eggplant salad topping that makes this a killer burger. Try the salad as a side dish on its own.

1 pound ground lamb

½ medium-size onion, finely chopped

2 cloves garlic, minced

2 tablespoons chopped fresh oregano leaves

2 tablespoons chopped fresh thyme leaves

1 teaspoon salt

½ teaspoon coarsely ground black pepper

1. Thoroughly knead all the ingredients together in a large mixing bowl until smooth, about 5 minutes. Form into 4 patties, each ½ inch thick.
2. Lightly oil the grill or a skillet over medium heat and cook the burgers to the desired degree of doneness, about 5 minutes per side for medium.

SERVE IT UP on toasted *ciabatta* bread or in toasted pita pockets

TOP IT OFF with Eggplant Feta Salad (recipe follows)

Eggplant Feta Salad

MAKES ABOUT 3 CUPS

Heap any extra salad into a pita pocket for a Greek-style vegetarian sandwich.

1 large eggplant, cut into ½-inch-thick rounds

1 medium-size zucchini, cut into ½-inch-thick rounds

1 large red onion, cut into ½-inch-thick rounds

1 tablespoon olive oil

Salt and coarsely ground black pepper to taste

½ cup crumbled feta cheese

2 scallions (white and green parts), thinly sliced

1 teaspoon chopped fresh thyme leaves

½ cup balsamic vinegar, reduced in a small saucepan over medium heat to ¼ cup

1. Place the eggplant, zucchini, and onion on a baking sheet. Drizzle with the olive oil and season with salt and pepper.
2. When ready to cook, lightly oil the grill or a grill pan over medium-high heat. Grill the vegetables until softened and lightly browned, 5 to 7 minutes for the eggplant and zucchini, 10 minutes for the onion. Turn often.
3. Transfer the vegetables to a large serving bowl. Add the feta and scallions and mix. Sprinkle with the thyme and drizzle with the vinegar reduction before serving.

KOFTE KEBAB BURGERS WITH CUCUMBER MINT SAUCE

MAKES 8 KEBABS, OR 4 SERVINGS

To the Arab world, *kofte* means "ground meat"—usually lamb—that is molded into flat cigar shapes and grilled on skewers. The garlicky Cucumber Mint Sauce doubles as a delicious salad dressing.

1 pound ground lamb

½ pound ground beef chuck

1 large onion, minced

¾ cup finely chopped fresh flat-leaf parsley leaves

1 clove garlic, minced

1 teaspoon ground cumin

1 teaspoon chili powder

1½ teaspoons salt

1 teaspoon coarsely ground black pepper

1. Combine all the ingredients in a large mixing bowl. Knead thoroughly for several minutes, squeezing the mixture through your fingers. You want a smooth texture.
2. Mold the mixture into 8 flat sausage shapes, each about 5 inches long and 2 inches wide.
3. Lightly oil the grill or a skillet over high heat and cook the kebabs until browned, 3 to 4 minutes per side.

SERVE IT UP **For each diner, place 2 of the kebabs in a toasted pita pocket.**

TOP IT OFF **with Cucumber Mint Sauce (recipe follows), chopped onion, and chopped fresh parsley**

Cucumber Mint Sauce

MAKES 1½ CUPS

This refreshing sauce also adds a cool zing to seafood burgers.

1 cup plain whole-milk yogurt

½ medium-size cucumber, peeled, seeded, and cut into ¼-inch dice

½ cup chopped fresh mint leaves

½ teaspoon salt

2 cloves garlic, minced

Mix all the ingredients together in a small bowl and serve.

HOME ON THE RANGE BUFFALO BURGERS WITH BROOKLYN KETCHUP

MAKES 4 BURGERS

Buffalo has a rich and robust taste—like beef, but with significantly less fat. Because it contains less fat than beef, buffalo also cooks a lot faster and is best when cooked medium rare. Overcooking will ruin its sweet juiciness and produce a dry, flavorless burger. Top it with the heavenly Brooklyn Ketchup—generously contributed by cookbook author and radio personality Arthur Schwartz, whose show, *Food Talk*, airs on WOR 710 AM radio in New York City.

1 pound ground buffalo meat (see Ingredient Sources, page 229)

1 clove garlic, minced

1 tablespoon ketchup

1 teaspoon Worcestershire sauce

½ teaspoon salt

¼ teaspoon coarsely ground black pepper

1. In a medium-size mixing bowl, gently mix together all the ingredients. Form into 4 patties, each ¾ inch thick.
2. Lightly oil the grill or a skillet over medium-high heat and cook the burgers to the desired degree of doneness, 1½ to 2 minutes per side for medium rare.

SERVE IT UP on toasted sesame seed buns

TOP IT OFF with Brooklyn Ketchup (recipe follows)

Brooklyn Ketchup

MAKES ABOUT 1/4 CUP

This is what "The Food Maven," Arthur Schwartz, says about ketchup: "I look forward to that particular hamburger experience so much—the meat juices and the ketchup mingling together and soaking into the soft bun—that I wouldn't think of using anything but ketchup. . . . This following concoction is merely a more piquant, more pronounced sweet-and-sour ketchup experience."

¼ cup ketchup

1 tablespoon cider vinegar

½ teaspoon dark brown sugar

1 clove garlic, minced

1 teaspoon Worcestershire sauce

2 to 6 drops Tabasco sauce, to your taste

In a small bowl or cup, beat all the ingredients together with a fork. If you let the ketchup stand for an hour or so, or up to 1 day, the garlic flavor becomes more pronounced. Schwartz advises that after 24 hours, the mixture might take on an unpleasant "off" garlic flavor. Keep it refrigerated.

BARBECUE, N'EST-CE PAS?

Barbecue is very American, but the origins of the word *barbecue* remain a mystery. It might be derived from the Caribbean Indian word *barbacoa*, a meat-smoking device. But it also might have originated with the French *barbe à queue*, or "whiskers to tail." Indian or French, American or not, it's mighty good eating!

BETTAH BUTTAH BURGERS

MAKES 4 BURGERS

Fantasizing about extra-juicy, extra-flavorful burgers? If so, this is the ticket. The secret is a disk of flavored butter that's tucked into the middle of the burger before it's cooked. You get mouthfuls of wonderful, buttery juiciness. We've created four flavored butters for you to choose from.

1½ pounds ground meat (beef, lamb, pork, turkey—whatever your pleasure)

2 teaspoons salt

1 teaspoon coarsely ground black pepper

4 to 6 tablespoons flavored butter (recipes follow), to your taste

1. Gently combine the meat, salt, and pepper in a large bowl. Form into 4 patties, each ¾ inch thick. With your thumb, make an indentation ½ inch deep and 2 inches wide in the center of each patty. Place at least 1 tablespoon of the flavored butter in the hole and pinch it closed.
2. Lightly oil the grill or a skillet over medium-high heat and cook the burgers to the desired degree of doneness, 3 to 5 minutes per side for medium rare.

SERVE IT UP on hamburger buns

TOP IT OFF with lettuce and sliced tomato

Pesto Butter

MAKES 1½ CUPS

1 cup tightly packed fresh basil leaves

4 cloves garlic, smashed

½ cup (1 stick) unsalted butter, softened

¾ cup freshly grated Parmesan cheese

2 teaspoons salt

Place the basil and garlic in a food processor and pulse until finely chopped. Add the remaining ingredients and process until smooth and well combined.

Triple-Pepper Butter

MAKES ½ CUP

½ cup (1 stick) unsalted butter, softened

2 teaspoons salt

1 teaspoon coarsely ground black pepper

1 teaspoon ground white pepper

½ teaspoon red pepper flakes, or more to taste

1 teaspoon ground cumin

1 teaspoon garlic powder

Combine all the ingredients in a food processor and pulse until smooth and well combined.

French Herb Butter

MAKES ½ CUP

½ cup (1 stick) unsalted butter, softened

3 large shallots, minced

2 tablespoons chopped fresh tarragon leaves

2 tablespoons chopped fresh thyme leaves

2 tablespoons chopped fresh flat-leaf parsley leaves

2 teaspoons salt

In a small mixing bowl, blend all the ingredients together until smooth and well combined.

Wasabi Butter

MAKES ½ CUP

½ cup (1 stick) unsalted butter, softened

2 scallions (white and green parts), minced

2 tablespoons wasabi paste or 1 tablespoon wasabi powder mixed with 1 tablespoon water

2 tablespoons soy sauce

In a small mixing bowl, blend all the ingredients together until smooth and well combined.

WHITE CASTLE TRIVIA

- In 1921, White Castle opened in Wichita, Kansas, offering hamburgers at 5 cents apiece. It was the world's first hamburger chain.
- White Castle served steam-grilled hamburgers, cooked on a bed of chopped onion. These square mini-burgers are called Slyders.
- It operates more than 310 restaurants in the Midwest and Northeast, plus Kentucky and Tennessee.
- It has served more than 12 billion hamburgers.
- White Castle now sells more than 500 million hamburgers a year.

Grilled Mustard Dill Turkey Burgers ❂ Tuscan Turkey Burgers with Balsamic Tomato Glaze ❂ Bolognese Turkey Burgers with Sun-Dried Tomatoes and Green Olives ❂ Cumin-Scented Turkey Burgers with Orange Chipotle Sauce ❂ Pecan Pesto Turkey

Burgers That Take Flight:

Burgers with Caramelized Fennel ❂ Braised Fajita Turkey Burgers with Fiesta Corn Salsa ❂ Tex-Mex Cheddar Turkey Burgers with Caramelized Onions ❂ Middle Eastern Turkey Kibbeh Burgers ❂ Asian Turkey Burgers ❂ Chicken Sausage Burgers ❂ Chicken and Turkey Paprikash Burgers ❂ Chicken Satay Burgers with Peanut Sauce and Spicy Cucumber Salad ❂ Chicken Marsala Burgers ❂ Curried Chicken Burgers ❂ Chili Chicken Burgers ❂ Hoisin Five-Spice Chicken Burgers with Carrot Daikon Slaw ❂ Breakfast Burgers with Rick Bayless's Roasted Jalapeño

Turkey, Chicken, and Duck

Tomato Salsa ❂ Herbed Chicken Burgers with Cranberry Horseradish Sauce ❂ Japanese Rice Burgers with Chicken Teriyaki ❂ Duck Burgers with Wild Rice Pancakes ❂ Jamaican-Spiced Ostrich Burgers

Poultry refers to any fowl raised for food, and there are plenty to pick from: chicken, turkey, duck, ostrich, pigeon, pheasant, goose, quail, partridge, or guinea fowl. Our burger recipes mostly call for ground chicken or turkey, but be inventive and try your own substitutions. We've never heard of partridge burgers, but, hey, go for it!

A Good Buy

Turkey and chicken are cheap compared to most other meat, but that wasn't always the case. Up until World War II, only the affluent could afford to eat it, saving it for Sunday dinners and special celebrations. In fact, chicken was even considered a luxury.

The Battle of the Bulge

The number of people who favor chicken over red meat keeps growing. In 1980, Americans ate about 46 pounds of chicken per person a year. As we've tried to slim down and get healthy, that figure has skyrocketed. The average American now gobbles up about 84 pounds of chicken annually.

Chicken is good for your health—a source of protein and niacin. But you can also get very ill from it by ignoring crucial food safety rules. Proper handling will greatly cut the risk of getting salmonella poisoning. See page 92 for proper handling tips.

Hey, Big Bird!

We're not saving turkey just for the holidays anymore. We now eat turkey fajitas, turkey chili, turkey sandwiches, and, of course, turkey burgers all the time. In 1980, the average American ate about 10 pounds of turkey a year; that number is now up to 18 pounds.

This New World native was once prized for its rich flavor, but today's turkey is a gross distortion of what it used to be. U.S. turkeys are bred to produce as much white meat as possible. As a result, American turkeys have such huge breasts (where the white meat is) that they can't even get close enough to each other to mate. So most turkeys are artificially inseminated. All this in the name of white meat.

> ***"I wish the bald eagle had not been chosen as the representative of our country! The turkey is a much more respectable bird, and withal a true original native of America."***
>
> **Benjamin Franklin, writing to his daughter**

White meat is more tender but much drier than dark meat (and, in our estimation, less flavorful). The disproportionate amount of white meat is why so many turkeys are dry and tasteless. That is also why legions of Thanksgiving cooks must take special pains to avoid an overcooked bird. So use a combination of white and dark meat (we like a 1:1 ratio) for a juicy, flavorful turkey burger. The same goes for chicken.

Picking Your Poultry

Here are some tips for choosing the right bird.

- SKIN: Look for soft and supple skin; it shouldn't be bruised or torn. The color can range from creamy white to buttery yellow, depending on what the bird was fed.
- SMELL: Avoid chicken and turkey with an off odor.
- TOUCH: The package containing the poultry should not be full of liquid or feel sticky.
- COLOR: The color of a skinless chicken fillet should be peachy pink, turkey, pale pink.

Don't Run Afowl of the Rules

Proper handling is the most important step in avoiding salmonella poisoning.

- Keep chicken and turkey stored in the coldest part of the fridge.
- Never eat raw poultry (yuck!).
- Keep your work area scrupulously clean. Use warm soapy water to wash your cutting board, knives, utensils, and hands—anything that comes in contact with raw poultry. In cooking school, we'd rinse everything with a bleach solution, but you don't have to go to such extremes.
- Don't let raw chicken or turkey juice come in contact with the cooked stuff.
- Keep your poultry separate from the rest of your food to avoid cross-contamination.

See page 5 for more guidelines.

Cook Your Goose

We follow USDA suggestions to cook ground chicken and turkey to 165°F. This holds true for most other poultry, with the exception of duck. We think duck breast tastes wonderful medium rare, so take that into consideration when you are cooking duck burgers.

Chicken and turkey burgers made from white meat tend to be dry. Be sure to add more fat or liquid to the mixture, and remember that you can always mix in ground dark meat with the white or try using dark meat only.

Be inventive with your poultry burgers. Just be sure to follow the safety guidelines, and your burgers will rule the roost.

GRILLED MUSTARD DILL TURKEY BURGERS

MAKES 4 BURGERS

Sometimes a condiment works well as a mix-in ingredient, not just as a topping. Here, mustard goes into the burgers as well as on them. This recipe is lowfat, low-cal, and low-carb, but it's high in Scandinavian flavor. For a change of pace, use a different mustard or herb.

6 tablespoons Dijon mustard

6 tablespoons coarsely chopped fresh dill

¼ cup finely chopped shallots

1 pound ground turkey

2 tablespoons plain dry bread crumbs

1 large egg

Salt and coarsely ground black pepper to taste

1. In a small bowl, mix together the mustard, dill, and shallots. Transfer half that mixture to a medium-size mixing bowl and reserve the rest for topping.
2. Add the turkey, bread crumbs, and egg to the larger bowl and mix until just combined. Form the mixture into 4 patties, each about ½ inch thick. Season with salt and pepper.
3. Lightly oil the grill or a skillet over medium-high heat and cook the burgers to the desired degree of doneness, at least medium, about 4 minutes per side.

SERVE IT UP on multigrain bread

TOP IT OFF with the remaining mustard-dill mixture

TUSCAN TURKEY BURGERS WITH BALSAMIC TOMATO GLAZE

MAKES 6 BURGERS

The mixture of rosemary and balsamic vinegar evokes Italy's Chianti countryside. Think sun-kissed villas perched among vineyards and olive groves. Bring a little Italy to your outdoor grill or hibachi and make sure to use a good-quality balsamic vinegar. The rich, sweet taste is worth the investment. The glaze is a great alternative to ketchup and easily doubles as a tangy barbecue sauce for ribs.

BURGERS

2 pounds ground turkey

¼ cup chicken broth

½ cup minced shallots

2 tablespoons finely chopped fresh rosemary leaves

¼ cup tomato paste

2 tablespoons balsamic vinegar

BALSAMIC TOMATO GLAZE

2 tablespoons tomato paste

1 tablespoon balsamic vinegar

1 tablespoon chicken broth

1. To make the burgers, place all the ingredients in a large mixing bowl and thoroughly combine, using your hands. Form into 6 patties, each 1 inch thick.
2. To make the glaze, whisk all the ingredients together in a small bowl and set aside.

3. Lightly oil the grill or a skillet over medium-high heat. (These also can be broiled.) Cook the burgers on one side for 5 minutes, then turn and brush the glaze on the cooked side. Continue to cook to the desired degree of doneness, at least medium, 3 to 5 minutes.

SERVE IT UP on toasted onion rolls or focaccia

TOP IT OFF with extra balsamic tomato glaze

KETCHUP OF THE MONTH

Go to store.yahoo.com/ketchupworld/index.html, call 866-KETCHUP, or e-mail the Ketchupman at ketchupman@ketchupworld.com for an eye-popping selection of ketchup. International varieties include those from Pakistan and Germany. Other options are Hot n' Spicy, Rich & Luscious, Sugarless, Organic, and Kosher. Some of the store's latest ketchup offerings include Beasley's Jamaican Jerk, Desert Rose Cactus (made with prickly pear cactus), and mesquite. There's even a Ketch of the Month Club.

BOLOGNESE TURKEY BURGERS WITH SUN-DRIED TOMATOES AND GREEN OLIVES

MAKES 4 BURGERS

These burgers are bursting with the flavors of Emilia-Romagna, Italy's culinary heart. They boast two of the region's most famous foods: Parmesan cheese and balsamic vinegar. Serve on toasted semolina bread brushed with a little olive oil—*perfetto*!

1½ pounds ground turkey, half dark and half white meat

⅓ cup minced sun-dried tomatoes

2 tablespoons minced pitted green olives (preferably the large Cerignolas; see Ingredient Glossary, page 225)

1 tablespoon good-quality balsamic vinegar

¼ cup dry red wine

¼ teaspoon salt

¼ teaspoon coarsely ground black pepper

8 thin slices Parmesan cheese (see Note)

1. Place all the ingredients except the Parmesan in a large mixing bowl and thoroughly combine, using your hands. Form into 4 patties, each 1 inch thick.
2. Lightly oil the grill or a skillet over medium-high heat. (These also can be broiled.) Cook the burgers for 3 minutes, then turn and place 2 Parmesan slices on top of each. Continue to cook to the desired degree of doneness, at least medium, about 4 minutes more.

NOTE Use a vegetable peeler to get thin slices of cheese that melt beautifully and add rich flavor without a lot of fat.

SERVE IT UP on pan-toasted semolina bread or focaccia

TOP IT OFF with arugula tossed in Sherry Wine Vinaigrette (page 191) or Sun-Dried Tomato Chutney (page 195)

MAKE A DATE

June is National Turkey Lovers' Month.

CUMIN-SCENTED TURKEY BURGERS WITH ORANGE CHIPOTLE SAUCE

MAKES 6 BURGERS

Lavash is the oldest known bread in the Middle East. It's flat and unleavened, often dried and served as crispy crackers. It's perhaps most recognizable as the packaging for roll-up sandwiches. We think it's the perfect wrap for this savory burger. Here the exotic mixture of cumin and orange conjures up Morocco. But you don't need to travel that far for special ingredients. A short trip to your local supermarket will do.

2 pounds ground turkey

1 teaspoon ground cumin

¼ cup finely chopped orange zest (from about 1 large orange)

1 cup tightly packed fresh flat-leaf parsley leaves, finely chopped

1 cup chicken broth

1. Place all the ingredients in a large mixing bowl and thoroughly combine, using your hands. Form into 6 patties, each 1 inch thick.
2. Lightly oil the grill or a skillet over medium-high heat. (These also can be broiled.) Cook to the desired degree of doneness, at least medium, about 4 minutes per side.

SERVE IT UP wrapped in warm lavash

TOP IT OFF with Orange Chipotle Sauce (recipe follows) and iceberg lettuce leaves

Orange Chipotle Sauce

MAKES 1 CUP

Try this at Thanksgiving. It's heavenly with roast turkey.

2 canned chipotle chile peppers in adobo sauce with 1 teaspoon of the sauce

1 tablespoon tomato paste

1 tablespoon minced red onion

¼ cup orange juice

¼ cup orange marmalade

Place all the ingredients in a food processor and process until smooth.

PECAN PESTO TURKEY BURGERS WITH CARAMELIZED FENNEL

MAKES 6 BURGERS

Our version of pesto, that ubiquitous basil and pine nut sauce, uses neither basil nor pine nuts. Instead, cilantro and pecans create a potent alternative. Caramelizing the fennel enhances its anise flavor.

2 pounds ground turkey

½ cup Pecan Pesto (recipe follows)

2 tablespoons olive oil

4 cups fennel bulbs cut into thin strips

Salt and coarsely ground black pepper to taste

1. Put the turkey and pesto in a large mixing bowl and thoroughly combine, using your hands. Form into 6 patties, each ½ inch thick. Cover with plastic wrap and place in the refrigerator to firm up until ready to cook.
2. Meanwhile, heat the olive oil in a large skillet over medium heat. Add the fennel and cook, stirring, until softened, 6 to 8 minutes. Season with salt and pepper. Keep warm for topping.
3. Lightly oil the grill or a skillet over medium-high heat. (These also can be broiled.) Cook the burgers to the desired degree of doneness, at least medium, about 4 minutes per side.

SERVE IT UP on Italian rolls or focaccia

TOP IT OFF with the sautéed fennel strips

Pecan Pesto

MAKES ½ CUP

½ cup pecans

1 cup tightly packed fresh cilantro leaves

¼ cup olive oil

¼ teaspoon salt

1. Put the pecans in a food processor and process until finely chopped.
2. Add the cilantro, olive oil, and salt and process until a coarse paste forms.

HE SAYS, SHE SAYS

Only tom turkeys gobble.

Hen turkeys make a clicking noise.

BRAISED FAJITA TURKEY BURGERS WITH FIESTA CORN SALSA

MAKES 3 BURGERS, OR 6 SERVINGS

Okay, we're taking a little poetic license here with a burger that's not grilled or sautéed, but instead simmered in a tomato broth. Slice the burgers fajita style, at an angle, and serve in warm flour tortillas. The word *fajita* is derived from *faja*, the Spanish word for belt or sash, probably because of the strips of meat.

1 pound ground turkey

Salt and coarsely ground black pepper to taste

1 teaspoon olive oil

¼ cup tomato puree

½ cup chicken broth

1. Form the turkey into 3 patties, each about 1 inch thick, and season generously with salt and pepper.
2. Heat the olive oil in medium-size skillet over medium heat and cook the patties until well browned on both sides.
3. Add the tomato puree and broth, cover tightly, reduce the heat to low, and cook for 15 minutes.

SERVE IT UP place half a burger, sliced fajita style, in a warm flour tortilla

TOP IT OFF with some of the pan sauce and Fiesta Corn Salsa (recipe follows)

Fiesta Corn Salsa

MAKES 2½ CUPS

A tasty side dish for any southwestern or south-of-the-border meal.

1½ cups cooked corn kernels, drained

1 small red onion, finely diced

1 fresh jalapeño chile pepper, seeded and finely diced

½ pint grape tomatoes, quartered

½ cup tightly packed fresh cilantro leaves, finely chopped

2 tablespoons capers, drained

1 tablespoon olive oil

¼ teaspoon salt

Place all the ingredients in a medium-size mixing bowl and mix to combine.

TEX-MEX CHEDDAR TURKEY BURGERS WITH CARAMELIZED ONIONS

MAKES 4 BURGERS

These Southwest-inspired burgers pack a wallop of flavors: chili, red onion, and cilantro. But the real kicker is the chipotles, or smoked jalapeños. Leave them out if you don't want the heat. The onion is meltingly tender and takes on the flavor of the barbecue sauce. Try a mesquite-flavored sauce for a smoky flavor.

1 ¼ pounds ground turkey

1 tablespoon chili powder

1 teaspoon ground cumin

1 small red onion, chopped

¼ cup chopped fresh cilantro leaves

¼ cup minced canned chipotle chile peppers in adobo sauce

1 cup grated cheddar cheese, for topping

1. In a large mixing bowl, gently combine all the ingredients except the cheese, using your hands. Form into 4 patties, each ¾ inch thick.
2. Lightly oil the grill or a skillet over medium-high heat and cook the burgers to the desired degree of doneness, at least medium, 4 to 6 minutes per side.

SERVE IT UP wrapped like a burrito in warm flour tortillas

TOP IT OFF with Caramelized Onions (recipe follows) and the cheese

Caramelized Onions

MAKES ABOUT 2 CUPS

2 tablespoons olive oil

2 large onions, very thinly sliced

¼ teaspoon salt

¼ teaspoon coarsely ground black pepper

¼ cup beef broth

½ cup barbecue sauce

2 tablespoons balsamic vinegar

1. Heat the olive oil in a large skillet over medium-high heat. Add the onions, salt, and pepper and cook, stirring often, until the onions are browned, 7 to 10 minutes.
2. Add the broth, barbecue sauce, and vinegar. Reduce the heat to low and simmer until the sauce thickens, about 15 minutes.

MORE THAN TEXAS BULL

Burger lovers in Texas know there's more than just beef on the bun at Hut's Hamburgers in Austin, which offers buffalo, chicken, and veggie burgers as well. Traditional Texas condiments include hickory sauce, or you can go Tex-Mex with guacamole and chipotle chile mayo.

Hut's Hamburgers • 807 West 6th Street • Austin, TX 78703 • (512) 472-0693

www.hutshamburgers.citysearch.com

MIDDLE EASTERN TURKEY KIBBEH BURGERS

MAKES 8 BURGERS

Classic *kibbeh*, a meat or fish dish layered with onions and pine nuts, is the inspiration for this burger. There's a hint of sweetness from the mixed-in spices and zest in these rectangular patties, cut after the traditional baking. The slightly dry and crunchy texture serves as burger and bun. We suggest lifting off the cooked top layer and adding a dollop of yogurt mixed with shredded fresh mint and finely diced red onion and cucumber. It's the perfect complement.

1 tablespoon olive oil

1 medium-size yellow onion, finely chopped

½ cup pine nuts

½ cup fine-grind bulgur wheat

½ cup chicken broth

Grated zest of 1 orange

½ teaspoon ground coriander

½ teaspoon ground cinnamon

½ teaspoon salt

½ pound ground turkey

1 pound sweet Italian turkey sausage, casings removed

1. Preheat the oven to 350°F.
2. Heat the oil in a medium-size skillet over medium heat. Add the onion and cook, stirring, until translucent, about 1 minute. Remove from the heat and mix in the pine nuts. Set aside.

3. In a large mixing bowl, combine the bulgur, ¼ cup of the chicken broth, the zest, coriander, cinnamon, and salt. Add the ground turkey and the remaining ¼ cup broth and mix well.
4. Using the back of a tablespoon, spread the sausage in a 9 x 14-inch baking pan. Be careful to cover the entire bottom of the pan, leaving no holes and filling in the corners. Spread the onion mixture evenly over the sausage. Using your hands, spread the bulgur-turkey mixture on top. Bake until a nice crust forms, about 30 minutes.
5. Using a serrated knife and metal spatula, cut into 8 rectangular burgers.

TOP IT OFF with Cucumber Mint Sauce (page 81, replacing the garlic with ¼ cup finely diced red onion). Lift off the top layer of each burger, dollop with the sauce, and replace the top.

ASIAN TURKEY BURGERS

MAKES 4 BURGERS

The flavors of Chinese cuisine—sesame oil, garlic, and ginger—are reinvented in this hearty burger. This is a landlubber version of our Asian Tuna Burger (page 156)—just as delicious, but made a lot heftier for big appetites.

- 1¾ pounds ground turkey
- 1½ tablespoons toasted sesame oil (see Note)
- 6 cloves garlic, minced
- ¼ cup soy sauce
- 1 tablespoon peeled and minced fresh ginger
- ¼ cup finely chopped fresh cilantro leaves

1. Gently mix all the ingredients together in a large mixing bowl, using your hands. Form into 4 patties, each 1 inch thick.
2. Lightly oil the grill or a skillet over medium-high heat and cook the burgers to the desired degree of doneness, at least medium, about 4 minutes per side.

NOTE Toasted sesame oil can be found in many supermarkets and Asian grocery stores. Do not substitute light sesame oil.

SERVE IT UP on toasted sesame seed buns

TOP IT OFF with Wasabi Mayo (page 157) or Orange Snow Pea Salad (page 181)

CHICKEN SAUSAGE BURGERS

MAKES 6 BURGERS

This is the quickest, easiest burger recipe we have. All you need is sausage and some oil. Just put the two in a pan (the burgers hold together better and stay moister when pan-fried rather than grilled) and, *voilà*—dinner! Many grocers carry an assortment of freshly made sausages filled with herbs and flavorful ingredients. This rendition was made with ground chicken mixed with scallion greens, bits of cilantro, and seasonings. You can always mix in your own herbs, sun-dried tomato bits, or cheese.

2 pounds chicken sausages

1 teaspoon vegetable oil

1. Remove the sausage meat from the casings and place in a large mixing bowl. Form into 6 patties, each 1 inch thick.
2. Heat the vegetable oil in a large skillet over medium-high heat and sear the burgers for about 1 minute on each side. Reduce the heat to medium-low and pan-fry until cooked all the way through, turning once, 8 to 10 minutes.

SERVE IT UP on toasted sesame seed buns or onion rolls

TOP IT OFF with lettuce, sliced tomato, and Dijon mustard

PRESIDENTIAL BURGERMEISTER

Richard M. Nixon, as a young naval officer in World War II, set up the only hamburger stand in the South Pacific. Nixon's Snack Shack served free burgers and Australian beer to flight crews.

CHICKEN AND TURKEY PAPRIKASH BURGERS

MAKES 6 BURGERS

Paprikash—"burger style." You may not be in Budapest, and there are no noodles involved, but the *paprikash* treatment is very apparent in this dish. And there's a heart-healthy bonus: this is a low-calorie version of the sauce, using yogurt instead of the more traditional fat-laden sour cream. Honestly, the strained yogurt makes for an imperceptible replacement.

1 pound ground chicken

1 pound ground turkey

½ cup seeded and finely diced red bell pepper

¼ cup finely chopped scallions (green part only)

1¾ cups chicken broth

1 tablespoon olive oil

1 medium-size red onion, thinly sliced

1½ teaspoons paprika

2 cloves garlic, minced

1 tablespoon tomato paste

1 tablespoon all-purpose flour

½ teaspoon salt

¼ teaspoon coarsely ground black pepper

1 cup plain lowfat yogurt, strained through a coffee or yogurt filter or a double thickness of cheesecloth for at least 1 hour

2 tablespoons finely chopped fresh flat-leaf parsley leaves

1. In a large mixing bowl, combine the ground chicken and turkey, bell pepper, scallions, and ¼ cup of the broth. Form into 6 patties, each ¾ inch thick, and refrigerate while you make the sauce.
2. Heat the oil in a large skillet over medium heat. Add the onion and cook, stirring, until translucent and just beginning to brown (but not burn), 3 to 5 minutes. Add the paprika and garlic, stir to combine, and turn off the heat. Add the tomato paste and flour and stir to combine.
3. Return the mixture to medium heat. Add the remaining 1½ cups broth, the salt, and pepper and cook for 5 minutes, stirring frequently. Turn off the heat. Add the yogurt and mix in thoroughly. Stir in the parsley.
4. Return the pan to medium-low heat and cook for 1 to 2 minutes, stirring constantly. Add the burgers and simmer until cooked all the way through, 8 to 10 minutes per side.

SERVE IT UP on toasted hamburger buns

TOP IT OFF with some of the pan sauce

TOP THIS

Ketchup isn't just for burgers. Here's how it's used around the world: Sweden, on pasta; eastern Europe, on pizza; Japan, on rice; Denmark, on spaghetti; Thailand, as a dip for potato chips; Great Britain, on fish and chips; Spain and India, on eggs.

CHICKEN SATAY BURGERS WITH PEANUT SAUCE AND SPICY CUCUMBER SALAD

MAKES 4 BURGERS

This exotic chicken burger is everything at once: sweet, hot, sour, and salty—very Southeast Asian. The secret ingredient to this burger's incredible taste? Peanut butter! You can barely taste it, but that's what unifies all the flavors. Serve with the peanut sauce for extra peanut punch.

2 tablespoons chunky or smooth peanut butter

2 teaspoons sugar

2 teaspoons Tabasco sauce

¼ cup chicken broth

1 pound ground chicken

1 tablespoon minced garlic

½ cup chopped fresh cilantro leaves

¼ cup chopped fresh mint leaves

½ teaspoon salt

1. Mix the peanut butter, sugar, Tabasco, and chicken broth together in a small bowl until well blended. Set aside.
2. In a large mixing bowl, mix together the ground chicken, garlic, cilantro, mint, and salt, using your hands. Add the peanut butter mixture and mix until combined. Form into 4 patties, each 1 inch thick.
3. Lightly oil the grill or a skillet over medium-high heat and cook the burgers to the desired degree of doneness, at least medium, about 4 minutes per side.

SERVE IT UP **on toasted sesame seed buns or wrapped in warm flour tortillas**

TOP IT OFF **with Peanut Sauce and Spicy Cucumber Salad (recipes follow)**

Peanut Sauce

MAKES ½ CUP

For an Asian pasta treat, coat cooked noodles with this sauce and serve hot or cold.

¼ cup chunky peanut butter
¼ cup chicken broth
2 teaspoons sugar
1 teaspoon red pepper flakes
1 teaspoon salt

Combine all the ingredients in a small bowl until well mixed and smooth.

Spicy Cucumber Salad

MAKES ABOUT 1½ CUPS

⅓ cup seasoned rice vinegar
1 tablespoon sugar
1 large cucumber, peeled, seeded, and cut into ¼-inch dice
½ teaspoon red pepper flakes
¼ teaspoon salt

1. In a medium-size mixing bowl, stir together the vinegar and sugar until the sugar dissolves. Add the cucumber, pepper flakes, and salt and stir to coat.
2. Let sit for at least 30 minutes before serving. Serve at room temperature.

CHICKEN MARSALA BURGERS

MAKES 6 BURGERS

This burger draws its inspiration from the classic Italian dish chicken Marsala. Mushrooms and shallots coax out the flavor of Marsala, a fortified wine from western Sicily. Use a good-quality Marsala, not the cooking variety, because if it's not good enough to drink, it's not good enough to cook with.

- **½ teaspoon all-purpose flour**
- **1 cup chicken broth**
- **1 tablespoon olive oil**
- **2 tablespoons minced shallots**
- **10 ounces white mushrooms, thinly sliced**
- **¼ cup plus 2 tablespoons dry Marsala**
- **¼ teaspoon salt**
- **⅛ teaspoon coarsely ground black pepper**
- **2 tablespoons finely chopped fresh flat-leaf parsley leaves**
- **2 pounds ground chicken**

1. In a small bowl, make a slurry by mixing the flour with ½ cup of the broth. Set aside.
2. Heat the olive oil in a large skillet over medium-high heat. Add the shallots and cook until translucent, about 1 minute. Reduce the heat to medium, add the mushrooms, and stir to combine with the shallots. Add ¼ cup of the broth and continue to cook for 5 minutes. Add ¼ cup of the Marsala, the salt, and pepper and continue to cook until the liquid is reduced by about three-quarters, 10 to 15 minutes. Stir in the parsley and slurry and transfer the mixture to a medium-size bowl.

3. In a large mixing bowl, combine the remaining 2 tablespoons Marsala into the ground chicken, using your hands. Form into 6 patties, each 1 inch thick. Place the burgers, together with the remaining ¼ cup broth, in the same skillet and cook over medium-low heat for 15 minutes, turning occasionally.
4. Add the mushroom mixture to the skillet and continue to cook for 5 minutes more.

SERVE IT UP on toasted sesame seed buns or thickly sliced Italian country bread

TOP IT OFF with the mushroom mixture

FORKS DON'T CUT IT

In Gainesville, Georgia, the Chicken Capital of the World, eating chicken with a fork is against the law.

CURRIED CHICKEN BURGERS

MAKES 4 BURGERS

Surprisingly, there's no consensus on curry's origins. It's believed that it emerged during the British colonization of India. This burger version delivers a spicy after-kick, so if you prefer a milder taste, you might consider cutting the amount of curry powder in half. The broth-infused patties are a little loose when they're formed but cook up into firm burgers.

2 tablespoons olive oil

3 tablespoons minced shallots

1 tablespoon plus 1 teaspoon peeled and minced fresh ginger

1 pound ground chicken

¾ cup chicken broth

2 tablespoons curry powder

2 tablespoons chopped fresh flat-leaf parsley leaves

1 tablespoon tomato paste

½ teaspoon salt

½ cup plain lowfat yogurt

1. In a small skillet, heat 1 tablespoon of the oil over medium heat. Add 2 tablespoons of the shallots and the ginger and cook, stirring, for about 30 seconds, mixing to combine and coat with the oil. Be careful not to burn the shallots. Set aside.
2. In a medium-size mixing bowl, combine the ground chicken, ¼ cup of the broth, 1 tablespoon of the curry powder, the parsley, and cooked shallots and ginger. Form into 4 patties, each ¾ inch thick. Cover with plastic wrap and refrigerate while you prepare the sauce.

Jalapeño Crab Burgers with Mango Salsa, *page 162*

Barbecue Cheese Burgers, *page 20*

Asian Salmon Burgers, ***page 148***

Bolognese Turkey Burgers with Sun-Dried Tomatoes and Green Olives, *page 96*

Chicken Satay Burgers with Peanut Sauce and Spicy Cucumber Salad, ***page 112***

Andouille Bayou Burgers with Red Pepper Mayo, *page 66*

Dilled Chickpea Burgers with Spicy Yogurt Sauce, ***page 206***

Honey Mustard Pork Burgers on Cheddar Thyme Biscuits, ***page 60***

3. Heat the remaining 1 tablespoon oil in a large skillet over medium-low heat, add the remaining 1 tablespoon shallots and 1 tablespoon curry and cook, stirring, for about 30 seconds, until the shallots are just translucent and the curry has toasted a little. Add the remaining ½ cup broth, the tomato paste, and salt. Slowly mix in the yogurt and cook for 2 to 3 minutes. Add the burgers and simmer until cooked all the way through, 10 to 12 minutes per side.

SERVE IT UP on lightly toasted hamburger buns

TOP IT OFF with the pan sauce

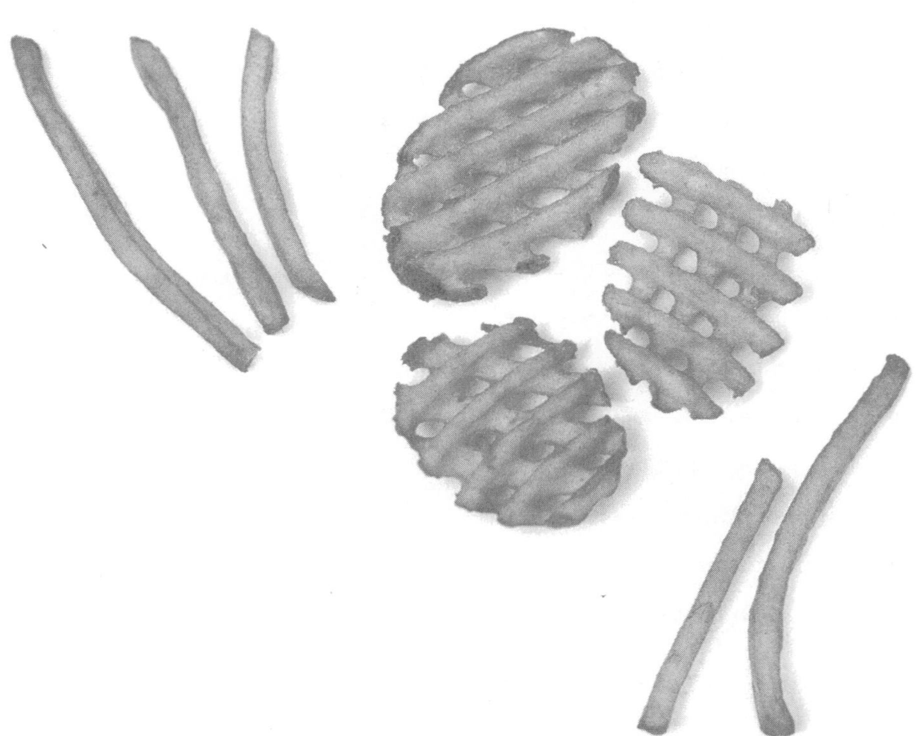

CHILI CHICKEN BURGERS

MAKES 4 BURGERS

Here chili goes in the burger and on top. And there's a bonus: the recipe makes enough chili mixture to accommodate doubling the number of burgers or to serve as a great leftover side dish or veggie meal on its own. Taste-test the chili topping so that you can add more spice if you want to crank it up a notch.

1 tablespoon olive oil

1 small yellow onion, finely chopped

¼ cup finely diced tomatillo

¼ cup seeded and finely diced fresh jalapeño chile peppers

2 teaspoons finely chopped fresh oregano leaves

3 tablespoons chili powder

¼ teaspoon salt

⅛ teaspoon coarsely ground black pepper

1¼ cups canned crushed tomatoes

One 15-ounce can black beans, rinsed and well drained

¼ cup chopped fresh cilantro leaves

1 pound ground chicken

1 tablespoon tomato paste

1 teaspoon turmeric

¼ cup chicken broth

1. Heat the oil in a large skillet over medium heat. Add the onion and cook, stirring, until just translucent, about 1 minute. Add the tomatillo, jalapeños, oregano, 2 tablespoons of the chili powder, the salt, pepper, 1 cup of the crushed tomatoes, and the beans and cook over medium-low heat for 5 to 7 minutes, stirring a few times. Add the cilantro. Keep warm for topping.

2. In a medium-size mixing bowl, combine the ground chicken, tomato paste, turmeric, broth, and remaining 1 tablespoon chili powder. Mix well and form into 4 loosely shaped patties, each ¾ inch thick.

3. Oil and preheat the grill (use a barbecue grate to support the patties) or a skillet over medium heat and cook the burgers to the desired degree of doneness, at least medium, 4 to 5 minutes per side.

SERVE IT UP on lightly toasted hamburger buns

TOP IT OFF with the chili mixture and lettuce leaves

BURGERS ARE ELEMENTARY AT THIS HARVARD INSTITUTION

For more than 40 years, Mr. Bartley's Burger Cottage has been serving up its unique, hand-formed burgers to academics and philistines alike. Sauces range from down-and-dirty barbecue to refined béarnaise and hollandaise. Bartley's also has a list of celebrity burgers, including the Elvis, the Bill Clinton, the Stephen King, and the Tiger Woods.

Mr. Bartley's Burger Cottage • 1246 Massachusetts Avenue
Cambridge, MA 02138 • (617) 354-6559
www.mrbartleys.com

HOISIN FIVE-SPICE CHICKEN BURGERS WITH CARROT DAIKON SLAW

MAKES 6 BURGERS

Short on time but tired of the same old burger? These quick-to-fix patties are animated with Asian ingredients. Slather a little extra hoisin sauce on your cooked burgers, along with the slaw topping. The slaw features daikon, a Japanese white radish with a mild bite. The Sakurajima, a related variety, can weigh as much as 50 pounds. (Just thought we'd throw in that curious tidbit for you to chew on while you chew on your burger.)

2 pounds ground chicken

2 tablespoons Chinese five-spice powder

2 tablespoons hoisin sauce, plus more for topping

¼ cup plus 2 tablespoons finely chopped cut scallions (green part only)

1. In a large mixing bowl, combine all the ingredients well. Wet your hands, then form the mixture into 6 patties, each about 1 inch thick.
2. Lightly oil the grill or a skillet over medium-high heat and cook the burgers to the desired degree of doneness, at least medium, 4 to 5 minutes per side.

SERVE IT UP wrapped in large lettuce leaves, or warm *moo shu* pancakes (see Ingredient Glossary, page 227), or warm flour tortillas

TOP IT OFF with extra hoisin sauce and Carrot Daikon Slaw (recipe follows)

Carrot Daikon Slaw

MAKES ABOUT 2¼ CUPS

An exotic riff on an all-American picnic favorite.

1 cup grated carrot

1 cup peeled and grated daikon

½ cup thinly sliced leeks (white part only)

1 tablespoon rice vinegar

1 tablespoon toasted sesame oil

½ teaspoon salt

1. In a medium-size mixing bowl, combine the carrot, daikon, and leeks.
2. In a small bowl, whisk together the vinegar, oil, and salt. Pour over the vegetable mixture and toss until evenly coated.

CARROTS HAVE DEEP ROOTS

Carrots are more than 3,000 years old. They were originally grown in Afghanistan and eventually made their way to the Mediterranean.

BREAKFAST BURGERS WITH RICK BAYLESS'S ROASTED JALAPEÑO TOMATO SALSA

MAKES 4 BURGERS

Here's a wake-me-up treat to start off your day on a delicious note—and a perfect use for leftover sausage. Use an egg ring, even a round cookie cutter, for shaping your burgers in the pan. Rick Bayless's salsa adds a mouthwatering zing to this breakfast burger.

½ small yellow onion, finely chopped and lightly sautéed in olive oil

1 ½ cups packed finely diced cooked chicken sausage meat

½ teaspoon salt

¼ teaspoon coarsely ground black pepper

2 large eggs, lightly beaten

1 tablespoon olive oil

1. In a large mixing bowl, combine all the ingredients except the oil.
2. Heat the oil in a large skillet over medium-high heat. Place one or more egg rings (or cookie cutters) in the skillet and fill each ring with about ½ cup of the burger mixture. Cook until firm, about 3 minutes. Remove the egg ring(s), flip the burger(s), and cook for another minute or so. Repeat with the remaining burger mixture.

SERVE IT UP on toasted English muffins

TOP IT OFF with Rick Bayless's Roasted Jalapeño Tomato Salsa (recipe follows)

Rick Bayless's Roasted Jalapeño Tomato Salsa

MAKES 5 CUPS

Rick Bayless's Chicago restaurants—Frontera Grill and Topolobampo—are temples of authentic Mexican cuisine. This cookbook author, teacher, and TV personality is also a king of salsa. He generously contributed this recipe for us to use on our burgers. According to Rick, "This classic home-style Mexican version of *salsa de molcajete* is made from garlic and roasted chiles pounded in a lava-rock mortar (*molcajete*) with roasted tomatoes." He suggests that other chile peppers, such as habanero and serrano, will work as well as the jalapeño. *Mmmmuy bueno.*

3 pounds ripe tomatoes (preferably plum)

4 to 6 fresh jalapeño chile peppers, to your taste, stemmed

1 small white onion, sliced ¼ inch thick and separated into rings

8 cloves garlic

⅔ cup loosely packed chopped fresh cilantro leaves

2 generous teaspoons salt

1 tablespoon cider vinegar

1. Preheat the broiler. Arrange the tomatoes and jalapeños on a baking sheet. Set the sheet 4 inches below the broiler, and broil until darkly roasted—even blackened—on one side (the tomato skins will split and curl in places), about 6 minutes. With a pair of tongs, flip over the tomatoes and jalapeños and roast for about 6 minutes more. The goal is not simply to char them, but to cook them through while developing a nice roasted flavor. Set aside.
2. Reduce the oven temperature to 425°F. On another baking sheet, combine the onion and garlic and place in the oven. Bake, stirring carefully every couple of minutes, until the onions are beautifully roasted (they'll be wilted, even slightly charred on some of the edges) and the garlic is soft and browned in spots, 15 to 20 minutes. Let cool to room temperature.

3. In a food processor, pulse the jalapeños with the onion-garlic mixture until moderately finely chopped, scraping everything down with a spatula as needed to keep it all moving around. Transfer to a large bowl.
4. Without washing the processor, coarsely puree the tomatoes and all the juice that has accumulated around them, then add them to the bowl. Stir in enough water (if you think it's needed—we didn't) to give the salsa an easily spoonable consistency (salsas in Mexico are usually a little smoother and saucier than they are here—not very chunky or thick). Stir in the cilantro, salt, and vinegar. Taste and adjust the seasonings. Remember, this condiment should be a little feisty. Use it right away or refrigerate, covered with plastic wrap, for up to 5 days.

TOMATO'S DAY IN COURT

Scientists today classify the tomato as a fruit. But in 1887, the U.S. Supreme Court ruled that the tomato is a vegetable and thus not subject to certain tariff restrictions on fruits.

HERBED CHICKEN BURGERS
WITH CRANBERRY HORSERADISH SAUCE

MAKES 6 BURGERS

Herbes de Provence **is the classic blend of dried herbs from southern France. You'll find it in the spice section of your grocery store. Make your own cranberry horseradish sauce by mixing together prepared horseradish and cranberry sauce to taste, or look for a prepared version, such as the one available from Stonewall Kitchen** **(see Ingredient Sources, page 230)****.**

2 pounds ground chicken

¼ cup minced shallots

2 tablespoons dried herbes de Provence

2 tablespoons chicken broth

Cranberry horseradish sauce (see headnote), for topping

1. In a large mixing bowl, combine all the ingredients except the sauce, using your hands. Form into 6 patties, each 1 inch thick.
2. Lightly oil the grill or a skillet over medium-high heat and cook the burgers to the desired degree of doneness, at least medium, 4 to 6 minutes per side, turning a few times.

SERVE IT UP on toasted egg bread or challah

TOP IT OFF with cranberry horseradish sauce

MISTAKEN IDENTITY

Contrary to popular belief, horseradish is not a member of the radish family but instead belongs to the mustard family.

JAPANESE RICE BURGERS WITH CHICKEN TERIYAKI

MAKES 2 BURGERS

Even die-hard classic burger fans have been converted by the famous MOS burger of Japan. It became an instant hit when the Japanese fast-food chain MOS introduced it. What is a MOS burger? It's a burger whose buns have been replaced with rice patties. The filling can be chicken, shrimp, vegetable, or beef, all slathered generously with teriyaki sauce. It's now one of the top sellers in Japan and across Asia. Here's our version.

½ cup panko (see Ingredient Sources, page 232) or plain dry bread crumbs

1 teaspoon monosodium glutamate (MSG)

Two 4- to 6-ounce chicken cutlets, trimmed of fat and skin and pounded ¼ inch thick

2 tablespoons canola oil

2 cups warm cooked short-grain white rice (see Note)

1. Combine the panko and MSG in a shallow bowl. Coat the cutlets evenly on both sides with the bread crumb mixture, tapping off any excess.
2. In a large nonstick skillet, heat 1 tablespoon of the oil over medium-high heat. Pan-fry the chicken cutlets until just cooked all the way through, 2 to 4 minutes per side. Remove from the heat and set aside.
3. To make the rice patties, take about ½ cup of the cooked rice and press it very tightly between the palms of your hands to make a patty ¾ inch thick. Make 4 patties.

4. Heat the remaining 1 tablespoon oil in a large nonstick skillet over medium-high heat. Pan-fry the rice patties until both sides are lightly golden, 1 to 3 minutes per side. Remove from the heat.

NOTE You must use short-grain rice so that it will stick together.

SERVE IT UP by placing each chicken cutlet on a rice patty.

TOP IT OFF with 1 tablespoon teriyaki sauce, 1 tablespoon salad dressing such as Miracle Whip, sliced tomato, and lettuce. Top with a second rice patty and serve immediately.

DUCK BURGERS WITH WILD RICE PANCAKES

MAKES 4 BURGERS

This is definitely a posh take on the humble burger. Your guests will think you fussed, but the dirty little secret is that this costs little time or money to make. The wild rice pancakes can be made ahead and even frozen for later use.

¼ pound duck breast fat

1 pound duck breast meat

2 tablespoons minced shallots

1 tablespoon finely chopped fresh thyme leaves

½ cup chicken broth

1 tablespoon chicken glace (see Ingredient Sources, page 229)

1 tablespoon tomato paste

¼ cup port

½ teaspoon salt

1. In a food processor, process the fat, then add the meat and chop to a "burger grind" consistency. Transfer to a large mixing bowl. Mix in the shallots and thyme. Wet your hands to help keep the meat from sticking, and form the mixture into 4 patties, each ½ inch thick.
2. Lightly oil a skillet over medium-high heat and sear the burgers for 3 minutes. Flip and cook for 5 minutes more. Transfer to a plate.
3. Reduce the heat to medium-low and deglaze the pan with ¼ cup of the broth. Add the glace, tomato paste, port, and salt and cook until reduced to a syrupy consistency, 10 to 15 minutes.
4. Return the burgers to the skillet, add the remaining ¼ cup broth, and cook over low heat for 10 to 15 minutes, turning to coat the burgers with sauce.

SERVE IT UP wrapped in Wild Rice Pancakes (recipe follows)

TOP IT OFF with the pan sauce

Wild Rice Pancakes

MAKES 8 PANCAKES

These pancakes are all about going fancy without the fuss.

1 cup cooked wild rice

1 cup all-purpose flour

1 ½ teaspoons baking powder

½ teaspoon salt

1 cup milk

1 extra-large egg, separated

1. In a large mixing bowl, combine the rice, flour, baking powder, and salt.
2. In a medium-size mixing bowl, whisk together the milk and egg yolk. Add to the rice mixture and mix well.
3. In another medium-size mixing bowl, with an electric mixer whip the egg white until stiff peaks form, then fold it into the rice mixture.
4. Heat and lightly oil a large nonstick griddle or skillet over medium-high heat. Drop ladlefuls of batter, about 2 tablespoons each, onto the griddle. Using the back of the ladle, gently spread the batter to make flat rounds. Cook until nicely browned, about 2 minutes. Flip and cook for 1 minute more. Serve hot.

NOTE **You can make these ahead and reheat, wrapped in aluminum foil. You can even freeze them for future use.**

JAMAICAN-SPICED OSTRICH BURGERS

MAKES 4 BURGERS

Ostrich is technically considered poultry, but it's cooked like venison, a lean red meat. Ostrich meat is beefy tasting, but it's also very lean and high in iron, and it contains half the calories of beef. These burgers will be darker in color than beef, and because ostrich contains very little fat, you must watch the cooking time very carefully, or you'll end up with dry, tough burgers.

1 pound ground ostrich meat (see Ingredient Sources, page 232)

1 clove garlic, minced

1 ½ tablespoons olive oil

1 ½ teaspoons salt

½ teaspoon coarsely ground black pepper

1 tablespoon onion powder

1 ½ teaspoons sugar

1 teaspoon dried thyme

½ teaspoon ground allspice

¼ teaspoon ground cinnamon

¼ teaspoon cayenne pepper

Pinch of ground ginger

1. In a medium-size mixing bowl, gently combine all the ingredients. Form into 4 patties, each ¾ inch thick.
2. Lightly oil the grill or a skillet over medium-high heat and cook the burgers to the desired degree of doneness, 3 to 5 minutes per side for medium rare.

SERVE IT UP on toasted sesame seed buns

TOP IT OFF with lettuce and sliced tomato

A NEW YORK INSTITUTION STAYS ITS GROUND

The relatively squat P. J. Clarke's building wasn't for sale, so developers built around it. Now surrounded by skyscrapers, this recently renovated New York City landmark is still serving its famous burgers in its carved oak and mirrored bar. Nat "King" Cole reportedly called the bacon cheeseburger the Cadillac.

P. J. Clarke's, once frequented by celebs such as Frank Sinatra and Jackie Onassis, was legendary for stargazing. Louis Armstrong is said to have played his trumpet in the back room while just hanging out.

P. J. Clarke's • 915 Third Avenue • New York, NY 10022 • (212) 317-1616

Apple Fennel Bluefish Burgers with Green Dijon Sauce ❂ Bluefish Burgers with Roasted Yellow Pepper Sauce ❂ My, My! Mahi Mahi Burgers with Tomato and Leek Salad ❂ Salmon Burgers in Grape Leaves ❂ Shelley's Salmon Croquette Burgers ❂

Gone Fishin' Burgers: Fish, Crab,

Salmon Bobotie Burgers ❂ Asian Salmon Burgers ❂ Scrod Burgers with Pear and Radicchio Poppy Seed Slaw ❂ Snapper Hash Burgers with Romesco Sauce ❂ Smoked Trout Burgers with Horseradish and Ricotta ❂ Legal Sea Foods Tuna Burgers ❂ Asian Tuna Burgers with Wasabi Mayo ❂ Tuna Shiso Burgers with Asian Salsa

❂ Conch Burgers ❂ Jalapeño Crab Burgers with Mango Salsa ❂ Caribbean Crab Burgers with Papaya Chutney ❂ Laurie's Dungeness Crab Burgers with Sweet Roasted Pepper Rouille ❂ Crawfish Pork Burgers with Scallion Mayonnaise ❂ Lobster Burgers

Lobster, Scallops, and Shrimp

with Hearts of Palm and Sauce Verte ❂ Woo You Oyster Burgers ❂ Scallop Burgers with Celeriac and Spicy Mayo ❂ Scallop and Cod Quenelle Burgers with Velouté Sauce ❂ Shrimp and Eggplant Burgers with Orange Snow Pea Salad ❂ Shrimp Gumbo Burgers ❂ Shrimp and Fennel Burgers ❂ Thai Shrimp and Crab Burgers

Crab cakes! Tuna burgers! Salmon croquettes! What do they have in common? They are all fish cakes—or, as we like to call them, burgers from the sea. Whether they're made from sweet, briny scallops or buttery salmon, fish cakes celebrate the ocean's bounty. They're also the frugal gourmet's best friend—the perfect way to use up leftover fish or to stretch pricey lobster to serve six.

A Healthy Body

Americans are eating more seafood than ever—about 15 pounds per person a year. In fact, fish consumption jumped in the 1990s after scientists found that fish is good for your heart. It contains cholesterol-lowering omega-3 fatty acids, which have been found to cut the risk of heart disease. And fish contains fewer calories, less cholesterol, and less fat than red meat.

Fresh Looks

Fresh fish has been highly prized since ancient times. The Incas had relay runners who raced up the mountains to Cuzco for deliveries, while Louis XIV had horse carts rush fresh fish to him at Versailles.

We have it much easier now, but we still want the freshest fish and shellfish possible, especially when it comes to making burgers. Here's what to check for.

- A clean, fresh ocean smell. Fish should not smell fishy.
- Firm flesh. It should bounce back when you press on it.
- Unblemished, moist, translucent flesh. It should have no dark spots or bruises. Fresh tuna and swordfish, however, often are sold with dark spots that can be cut out. The flesh should be shiny, not slimy or dried out.
- If you are buying whole fish, the eyes should be clear, the scales intact, and the gills red, not gray. Only a few fish, such as walleye, have naturally cloudy eyes.

Follow the same basic criteria when choosing shrimp and scallops. For other shellfish, here's what to look for.

- Crabs and lobsters should be lively and react when you pick them up. The lobster's tail should curl under.
- Clams, oysters, and mussels should have tightly closed shells. If they are slightly opened, they should close if you tap on them. Avoid broken or empty shells and shells that are unusually heavy. Discard any mollusks that don't open when cooked.
- When buying picked crabmeat or precooked packaged lobster meat, make sure to check the expiration date.

Here are some other general tips about buying fish.

- Buy from a reputable fishmonger who knows where the fish comes from. Shopping at seafood stores usually ensures a high turnover of fish—another good indicator of freshness.
- Seafood should be displayed on fresh—not melting—ice. It should not be submerged in any kind of liquid.
- Avoid cooked seafood that is placed next to the raw stuff. You want to avoid cross-contamination of bacteria. (See page 5 for information on safe food handling.)
- Fish handlers should wear rubber or plastic gloves.

So Many Fish, So Little Time

There really is an ocean of possibilities, considering that there are more than 20,000 kinds of fish and shellfish in the world, and most of them make great burgers. Remember, our recipes are merely a guideline (and hopefully an inspiration). If you don't want salmon, substitute another moderately fatty fish such as arctic char (a salmon relative) or pompano. Use the following chart to help you choose.

FISH SUBSTITUTION OPTIONS

LEAN	MODERATELY FATTY	FATTY
Catfish	Amberjack	Buffalo fish
Cod	Arctic char	Eel
Flounder	Bluefish	Herring
Grouper	Butterfish	King salmon
Halibut	Carp	Sablefish
Mahi mahi	Mackerel	Shad
Orange roughy	Mullet	Turbot
Salmon*	Pompano	Whitefish
Sea bass	Salmon	Yellowtail
Snapper	Sturgeon	
Sole	Tuna (albacore, bonito)	
Striped bass		
Swordfish		
Tilapia		
Trout (brook, rainbow)		
Tuna (bigeyed, bluefin, skipjack, yellowfin)		
Walleye		

* Only chum and pink salmon are lean. All other salmon are moderately fatty.

Keep It All Together

One concern in cooking fish burgers is that they tend to fall apart. Here are a few tips to keep it together.

- Add more bread crumbs if your burger mixture is looking too loose (but be careful not to overdo it).
- Use a ¼- or ½-cup measure and pack your burger mixture in the cup to form a firmer patty.

- Refrigerate your burgers for 30 minutes to 2 hours before cooking to help firm them up.
- Consider an extra egg or egg white or another binder, such as mayonnaise or yogurt, if the patties still haven't firmed up after they're refrigerated.

Most fish and shellfish burgers cook up better in a skillet. Since they tend to be more delicate than meat, they hold their shape better on a flat cooking surface with more careful handling. The subtle flavors of fish lend themselves to cooking in a pan, where they're enhanced, rather than being overwhelmed by the smoky flavor from a grill. There are exceptions, such as burgers made from "meatier" fish (tuna or salmon), which benefit from grilling. Most seafood burgers can be baked or broiled. The main thing is to avoid overcooking or burning them.

How Long to Cook It

Ah, the great debate! For safety reasons, the USDA suggests cooking fish to an internal temperature of 145°F. But the thought of rubbery shrimp or dried-out crab burgers makes us blanch! A general rule of thumb is 8 to 10 minutes per inch of thickness, or about 4 to 5 minutes per side.

The most important thing about cooking seafood, whether it's ground cod or a whole snapper, is this: *Do not overcook it.* If it's a bit underdone, you can always throw it back on the stove. But you can't uncook it once it's done.

Now start cooking those fish burgers!

TWO WAYS TO CHECK IF YOUR FISH BURGER IS READY

1. **Fish is done when it is opaque throughout.**
2. **Insert an instant-read thermometer in the thickest part of the burger. It's cooked through at 137°F. We like ours just done, at around 135°F. There are exceptions, of course. Many people like tuna and salmon a bit underdone, about 120°F.**

APPLE FENNEL BLUEFISH BURGERS WITH GREEN DIJON SAUCE

MAKES 4 BURGERS

Apple and fennel form the perfect backdrop for the assertive taste of bluefish. Together, they offer a sophisticated trio of flavors: sweet and savory, with a hint of licorice. Toasted sunflower seeds add a buttery crunch. Snapper would also work well here.

1 pound bluefish fillets, cooked (we suggest broiling them spritzed with the juice of 1 lemon)

3 tablespoons olive oil

1 medium-size fennel bulb, stalks discarded and cut into ¼-inch dice (about 1½ cups)

1 Granny Smith apple, peeled, cored, and cut into ¼-inch dice (about 1½ cups)

¼ teaspoon salt

¼ teaspoon coarsely ground black pepper

1 large egg, lightly beaten

¼ cup toasted hulled sunflower seeds, ground in a food processor

1. Put the bluefish in a large mixing bowl and mash well with a fork.
2. Heat 1 tablespoon of the olive oil in a large skillet over medium heat. Add the fennel and cook, stirring, until soft and golden, 5 to 7 minutes. Add the apple, salt, and pepper and cook, stirring, until the apple is soft and any liquid in the skillet has completely evaporated, 3 to 4 minutes.
3. Transfer the apple mixture to the bowl with the fish and combine. Add the egg and mix well. Form the mixture into 4 patties, each ¾ inch thick. Dredge them evenly on all sides in the ground sunflower seeds.
4. Heat 1 tablespoon of the olive oil in a large skillet over medium heat and pan-fry 2 of the burgers until

browned on each side, 5 to 7 minutes total. Remove from the pan and keep warm in a low oven. Repeat with the remaining 2 burgers.

SERVE IT UP on multigrain rolls or warm herb bread

TOP IT OFF with Green Dijon Sauce (recipe follows) or Roasted Yellow Pepper Sauce (page 141)

Green Dijon Sauce

MAKES ½ CUP

You can also serve this mustard-based topper with Herbed Chicken Burgers (page 125).

¼ cup capers, drained

3 scallions (white and green parts), chopped

½ cup tightly packed fresh basil leaves

1 cup tightly packed fresh flat-leaf parsley leaves

2 tablespoons whole-grain Dijon mustard

¼ cup olive oil

Salt and coarsely ground black pepper to taste

1. Place the capers, scallions, basil, parsley, and mustard in a food processor and finely grind.
2. With the machine running, slowly pour the olive oil through the feed tube until the mixture attains a thick, sauce-like appearance. Season with salt and pepper.

BLUEFISH BURGERS WITH ROASTED YELLOW PEPPER SAUCE

MAKES 4 BURGERS

Bluefish get around. They're found all over the place—from Maine to Florida, in the coastal waters off Africa, and in parts of Europe, Malaysia, and Australia. And they've found their way here in a satisfying burger with a touch of mustard and topped with a mellow roasted pepper sauce. You can substitute grouper or pollock, if you wish.

1 lemon, halved

1 pound bluefish fillets

1 large egg

2 tablespoons plain yogurt

1 tablespoon Dijon mustard

2 scallions (white and green parts), finely chopped

2 teaspoons vegetable oil

1. Squeeze 1 lemon half over the fish and broil until tender, 2 to 4 minutes. Remove from the oven and squeeze the remaining lemon half over the fish.
2. Remove the skin and put the meat in a large mixing bowl. Mash with a fork into fine bits. Add the egg, yogurt, mustard, and scallions and mix thoroughly. To make the burgers, pack one-quarter of the mixture into a ½-cup measure and place the patty on a baking sheet. Repeat with the remaining mixture. Cover with plastic wrap and refrigerate for at least 1 hour to firm up.
3. Heat the vegetable oil in a large skillet over medium heat. Add the burgers and pan-fry until cooked through and a light crust forms on both sides, 2 to 4 minutes per side.

SERVE IT UP on toasted English muffins or focaccia

TOP IT OFF with Roasted Yellow Pepper Sauce (recipe follows) or Orange Basil Sauce (page 197)

Roasted Yellow Pepper Sauce

MAKES 3/4 CUP

2 medium-size yellow bell peppers

1 teaspoon olive oil

¼ teaspoon salt

¼ teaspoon coarsely ground black pepper

1. Roast the bell peppers by putting them directly over a gas flame or on a baking sheet under a preheated broiler, turning often so the skin chars evenly, 5 to 7 minutes. Remove from the heat, place in a bowl, and cover with plastic wrap. Let sit until cool enough to handle.
2. Remove the skins and seeds. Place in a blender along with the remaining ingredients and process until smooth.
3. Refrigerate for at least 2 hours, or up to overnight, for the flavors to develop.

YANKEES FANS GO CRAZY FOR MUSTARD

In an average year, Yankee fans consume 1,600 gallons of mustard, not including the 2 million packets they use.

MY, MY! MAHI MAHI BURGERS WITH TOMATO AND LEEK SALAD

MAKES 4 BURGERS

Mahi mahi is Hawaiian for "strong strong." This "strong" swimmer used to be called dolphinfish to distinguish it from the Flipper-like dolphin mammal. It's meaty and flaky and makes for a great burger. Juicy roasted peppers, tangy Parmesan, and cornmeal lend a Southwest accent to this burger. Be sure to cut the zucchini into very small dice so the patties hold together. Swordfish would work well as a substitute.

1 pound mahi mahi fillets, skin removed and cooked (we suggest broiling them spritzed with the juice of ½ lemon)

2 tablespoons olive oil

½ small red onion, finely diced

1 medium-size, slender zucchini, seeded and finely diced

1 roasted red pepper (from a jar), drained and finely chopped

¼ cup freshly grated Parmesan cheese (preferably Parmigiano-Reggiano)

½ teaspoon salt

½ teaspoon coarsely ground black pepper

1 large egg

½ cup cornmeal

1. Put the fish in a large mixing bowl and mash well with a fork.
2. Heat 1 tablespoon of the oil in a medium-size skillet over medium-high heat. Add the onion and cook, stirring, until softened, about 1 minute. Add the zucchini and cook, stirring occasionally, until softened, 3 to 4 minutes.

3. Transfer to the bowl with the fish. Add the roasted pepper, Parmesan, salt, pepper, egg, and cornmeal and mix well. Form the mixture into 4 patties, each 1 inch thick.
4. Heat the remaining 1 tablespoon oil in a large skillet over medium-high heat and cook the burgers until browned on both sides, 6 to 8 minutes total.

SERVE IT UP on English muffins or Honey Whole Wheat with Seeds from Amy's Bread (page 218)

TOP IT OFF with Tomato and Leek Salad (recipe follows) or Romesco Sauce (page 153)

Tomato and Leek Salad

MAKES ABOUT 4 CUPS

2 pints grape or cherry tomatoes

1 medium-size leek (white part only), washed well and sliced into thin rings

1 cup tightly packed fresh basil leaves

2 tablespoons olive oil

1½ tablespoons balsamic vinegar

Salt and coarsely ground black pepper to taste

½ cup chopped walnuts, toasted (see Note)

1. Cut the tomatoes into halves (to yield about 4 cups) and place in a large mixing bowl. Add the leeks.
2. Cut the basil leaves into thin ribbons and add to the tomatoes and leeks.
3. In a small bowl, whisk together the olive oil, vinegar, salt, and pepper and toss with the vegetables to coat evenly. Add the walnuts, give a final toss, and serve immediately.

NOTE To toast nuts, preheat the oven to 350°F. Spread the nuts evenly on a baking sheet and toast until golden brown, about 5 minutes. Let cool before using.

SALMON BURGERS IN GRAPE LEAVES

MAKES 24 PACKETS, OR 8 SERVINGS

Grape leaves soaked in brine make wonderfully flavored wrappings for a variety of fillings, from fish (as in this salmon burger) to goat cheese. After grilling, wrap three salmon packets in a piece of lavash to make a hearty sandwich.

1 pound salmon fillets, skin and any bones removed

¼ cup minced shallots or red onion

2 tablespoons Dijon mustard

2 tablespoons soy sauce

¼ cup olive oil

24 grape leaves in brine, drained and patted dry

½ lemon

1. Finely chop the salmon by hand; a food processor will ruin the texture. Place in a medium-size bowl and add the shallots and mustard. Mix well.
2. In a small bowl, whisk together the soy sauce and olive oil.
3. Place 1 tablespoon of the fish mixture in the middle of a grape leaf and fold over as you would a burrito. Repeat with the remaining filling and leaves. Use a pastry brush to coat each packet with the soy-oil mixture.
4. Lightly oil the grill or a skillet over medium-high heat and cook the packets, squeezing the lemon over them, until slightly crispy, 5 to 7 minutes per side.

SERVE IT UP wrapped in warm lavash or stuffed into warm pita pockets

TOP IT OFF with extra Dijon mustard

SHELLEY'S SALMON CROQUETTE BURGERS

MAKES 4 BURGERS

We admit it: we're food snobs when it comes to fish. We'll choose fresh fish over canned any day. So we were somewhat skeptical when Shelley Greenberg, a friend of Liz's mom, told Liz about her salmon croquette burgers that used canned salmon. But wait! We swear these are the best salmon croquette burgers ever, and they are a cinch to make. Our hats are off to Shelley, who showed us the beauty of canned salmon.

One 7½-ounce can sockeye salmon, drained, picked over for cartilage and skin, and mashed

1 medium-size onion, finely grated

2 or 3 large eggs (2 eggs for a firmer burger, 3 eggs if you want a moister center)

½ cup seasoned dry bread crumbs

¼ cup canola oil

1. In a medium-size mixing bowl, combine the salmon, onion, eggs, and bread crumbs until well mixed.
2. Heat a large skillet over medium heat until hot, then add the oil. When the oil is hot but not smoking, ladle the mixture into the skillet to form 4 burgers. Cook until slightly browned, 2 to 3 minutes per side.

SERVE IT UP on toasted white or semolina bread

TOP IT OFF with mayonnaise and sliced tomato, or Dijon mustard and arugula

SALMON BOBOTIE BURGERS

MAKES 6 BURGERS

South African *bobotie* was originally a Malaysian creation. Traditionally, it's a bready custard-like meat loaf or meat pie made with ground lamb. Today there are recipes for poultry and fish versions as well. Here we offer a salmon interpretation, using the hallmark ingredients: curry powder, nuts, and fruit.

1 pound salmon fillets, skin and any bones removed and cut into small chunks

1 cup finely diced crustless white or semolina bread

½ cup milk

2 tablespoons olive oil

1 small yellow onion, finely chopped

2 tablespoons curry powder

1 large egg

½ teaspoon turmeric

2 tablespoons finely chopped slivered almonds

2 tablespoons dried currants

2 tablespoons fruit chutney

1. In a food processor, grind the salmon to a fine consistency. Place in a bowl and refrigerate.
2. In a small bowl, soak the bread in the milk for a few minutes, mashing it several times with a fork.
3. Heat 1 tablespoon of the oil in a medium-size skillet over medium-high heat. Add the onion, reduce the heat to medium, and cook until translucent, about 1 minute. Add the curry powder and cook for about 30 seconds, until the curry is fragrant and combined with the onion. Remove from the heat.

4. In a large mixing bowl, combine the ground salmon, soaked bread, egg, turmeric, almonds, currants, and chutney. Add the onion mixture and mix well. Using wet hands, form into 6 patties, each about ¾ inch thick.

5. Heat ½ tablespoon of the oil in a medium-size skillet. Add 3 of the patties and pan-fry just until cooked through, 3 to 5 minutes per side. Repeat with the remaining 3 patties.

SERVE IT UP on lightly toasted white bread or brioche

TOP IT OFF with extra chutney (if you like) and lettuce leaves

IT'S ALL IN THE FAMILY

Readers of the *Seattle Weekly* voted the Red Mill winner of the city's Best Burger. It's a family run operation, with brothers John and Michael Shepherd and their sister, Babe, at the helm. Favorites include the Bacon Deluxe with Cheese, the Verde Chicken Burger, the chicken club, and three different veggie burgers.

Red Mill Burgers • 312 North 67th Street • Seattle, WA 98103 • (206) 783-6362

ASIAN SALMON BURGERS

MAKES 4 BURGERS

The buttery richness of salmon rounds out the pungent seasonings of the oyster sauce in this burger. But you could substitute a less fatty fish, such as swordfish or tuna, for a variation. Serve with a crisp green salad and lemon ice for a luscious meal.

1 pound salmon fillets, skin and any bones removed

1 small onion, grated

2½ tablespoons Chinese oyster sauce

1. In a food processor, pulse the salmon until it resembles a coarse paste. Add the onion and oyster sauce and pulse just to combine. Transfer to a medium-size mixing bowl, cover with plastic wrap, and refrigerate for at least 30 minutes to firm up. Form into 4 patties, each ½ inch thick.
2. Heat a large nonstick skillet over high heat until smoking. Lightly coat it with nonstick cooking spray. Cook the salmon burgers until opaque all the way through, 2 to 4 minutes per side, or to the desired degree of doneness.

SERVE IT UP on toasted brioche or potato bread

TOP IT OFF with a squeeze of fresh lemon juice, a bit of oyster sauce, and thinly sliced red onion

LOOK, MA, NO HANDS!

It's against the law to catch fish with your bare hands in Kansas.

SCROD BURGERS WITH PEAR AND RADICCHIO POPPY SEED SLAW

MAKES 4 BURGERS

Guess what? Scrod doesn't actually exist as a type of fish per se. It's believed that a chef at Boston's Parker House invented the word to describe any cod, haddock, or pollock under 2½ pounds. This satisfying burger concoction of scrod and potatoes, flecked with bits of green zucchini, is a New England favorite. Be sure to check for any bones in the fish before mashing it with the potatoes.

1 pound scrod, cod, or haddock fillets, any bones removed

Juice of ½ lemon

6 small Yukon Gold potatoes, peeled

3 tablespoons olive oil

1 small onion, diced

1 cup seeded and diced zucchini

1 large egg, beaten

2 tablespoons sour cream

1½ teaspoons salt

½ teaspoon coarsely ground black pepper

⅓ cup seasoned dry bread crumbs

1. Place the scrod and lemon juice in a medium-size skillet. Add water to cover, place the lid on the skillet, and simmer over medium heat until the fish is opaque, about 5 minutes. Remove from the heat and drain. Set aside in a medium-size bowl.

2. Meanwhile, place the potatoes in a medium-size saucepan with water to cover. Bring to a boil and continue to boil until tender, 10 to 12 minutes. Drain, transfer to a large bowl, and mash.

3. Lightly mash the poached scrod and add to the potatoes.

4. In a medium-size skillet over medium heat, heat 1 tablespoon of the olive oil. Add the onion and zucchini and cook, stirring, until soft and golden, 5 to 7 minutes. Add to the scrod and potatoes, along with the egg, sour cream, salt, and pepper, and mix well. Shape the mixture into 4 patties, each 1 inch thick. Dredge evenly and on all sides in the bread crumbs.

5. Heat 1 tablespoon of the olive oil in a large skillet over medium heat. Add 2 of the burgers and pan-fry until browned on both sides and heated through, 4 to 5 minutes total. Remove from the pan and drain on paper towels. Repeat with the remaining 2 burgers.

SERVE IT UP on warm soft rolls or toasted hamburger buns

TOP IT OFF with Pear and Radicchio Poppy Seed Slaw (recipe follows)

Pear and Radicchio Poppy Seed Slaw

MAKES 4 TO 5 CUPS

Spiff up your slaws by adding fruit. If you like, try using a sweet apple instead of a pear in this rendition.

1 small head radicchio

1 medium-size, firm Bosc, Anjou, or Bartlett pear

⅓ cup plain yogurt

1 tablespoon mayonnaise (optional)

1 tablespoon sherry wine vinegar

½ teaspoon salt

¼ teaspoon coarsely ground black pepper

1 teaspoon poppy seeds

1. Slice the radicchio in half, cut out the core, and cut each half into thin strips.
2. Cut the pear in half and core. Slice thinly lengthwise, then slice crosswise into ¼-inch-wide strips.
3. Combine the radicchio and pear strips in a large salad bowl.
4. In a small bowl, combine the yogurt, mayonnaise (if using), vinegar, salt, and pepper. Toss with the slaw. Sprinkle the poppy seeds on top, toss lightly, and serve immediately.

SNAPPER HASH BURGERS WITH ROMESCO SAUCE

MAKES 6 BURGERS

This fish hash burger would make a great brunch dish, but it's hearty enough for a satisfying dinner as well. The delicate and sweet snapper gets a little comfort food heft from the potatoes. Bass or grouper would do the trick here, too.

5 tablespoons olive oil

1 medium-size yellow onion, finely diced

½ cup seeded and finely diced red bell pepper

½ cup seeded and finely diced green bell pepper

1 pound red snapper fillets, skin and any bones removed, then finely chopped

3 cups frozen hash brown potatoes, thawed

1 extra-large egg, lightly beaten

½ teaspoon salt

¼ teaspoon coarsely ground black pepper

1. Heat 1 tablespoon of the oil in a medium-size skillet over medium-high heat. Add the onion and cook, stirring, for 1 minute. Add the bell peppers and cook for 1 minute more. Remove from the heat.
2. In a large mixing bowl, combine the onion-pepper mixture with the chopped fish.
3. Wash or wipe out the skillet. Over medium-high heat, heat 2 tablespoons of the oil in the skillet. Add the potatoes and cook until lightly browned all over, 5 to 7 minutes. Add to the fish mixture along with the egg, salt, and pepper. To make the burgers, pack one-sixth of the mixture into a ½-cup measure and place the patty on a baking sheet. Repeat with the remaining mixture. Cover with plastic wrap and refrigerate for at least 30 minutes, or up to 2 hours, to firm up.

4. Heat 1 tablespoon of the oil in a medium-size skillet over medium-high heat. Add 3 of the burgers and reduce the heat to medium. Cook until a brown crust forms, 4 to 5 minutes, then flip and cook for 5 minutes more. Transfer to a platter and keep warm. Repeat with the remaining 3 burgers.

SERVE IT UP on sliced Italian country bread or toasted hamburger buns

TOP IT OFF with Romesco Sauce (recipe follows)

Romesco Sauce

MAKES ½ CUP

This is garlicky and spicy—a perfect topping for fish, chicken, or even beef.

2 tablespoons slivered almonds

One ½-inch-thick slice country bread, toasted and torn into pieces

2 cloves garlic, minced

One 7-ounce jar roasted red peppers, drained

1 ripe plum tomato, roasted (see Note) and coarsely chopped

1 tablespoon olive oil

1 tablespoon sherry wine vinegar

¼ teaspoon red pepper flakes

1. In a small skillet over medium heat, lightly toast the almonds, tossing frequently, until golden.
2. Place the almonds in a food processor with the bread and garlic. Process until the mixture is almost pulverized. Add the roasted peppers, tomato, olive oil, vinegar, and red pepper flakes and process until the mixture resembles a coarse puree.

NOTE **To roast a tomato, cut it in half lengthwise, remove the seeds, and place cut side down on a baking sheet. Broil until the skin is charred. Cool for 15 minutes and peel off the skin.**

SMOKED TROUT BURGERS WITH HORSERADISH AND RICOTTA

MAKES 6 BURGERS

These crowd-pleasing patties are our take on a New York deli favorite: smoked trout with red onion and horseradish. We've added ricotta cheese and topped them with green apple for a subtle creamy sweetness. These burgers are perfect if you're crunched for time because they need no cooking. We especially love them for Sunday brunch.

½ pound smoked trout, cut into small chunks

3 tablespoons prepared horseradish

½ cup ricotta cheese (fat-free works well)

1. Put the trout, horseradish, and ricotta in a food processor and pulse just to combine.
2. Transfer to a medium-size mixing bowl and continue to mix until all the ingredients are well blended. Form into 6 patties, each ½ inch thick.

SERVE IT UP on dark German pumpernickel bread

TOP IT OFF with thinly sliced green apple and thin strips of red onion

LEGAL SEA FOODS TUNA BURGERS

MAKES 8 BURGERS

"If it isn't fresh, it isn't Legal!" Legal Sea Foods claims that it's "not a restaurant company selling fish, but rather a fish company in the restaurant business." The company, which was started in Cambridge, Massachusetts, now has 26 locations along the eastern seaboard. Legal Sea Foods's tuna burger, contributed by executive chef Rich Vellante, is very user-friendly and a definite two-fisted pleaser.

3 pounds tuna, ground in a food processor

2 tablespoons chopped fresh flat-leaf parsley leaves

1 cup plain dry bread crumbs

1 tablespoon fresh lemon juice

1 teaspoon minced garlic

¾ cup grated asiago cheese

1 tablespoon fish sauce (available in Asian markets)

½ cup olive oil, plus more for grilling

1½ tablespoons Asian garlic chili paste (see Ingredient Sources, page 229)

¼ cup Sherry Wine Vinaigrette (page 191)

1. In a large mixing bowl, combine all the ingredients except the vinaigrette. Form into 8 patties, each about ½ inch thick.
2. Lightly oil the grill or a skillet over medium-high heat. Brush one side of the burgers with olive oil and grill, oil side down, for 3 to 4 minutes. Brush the other side of the burgers with oil, flip, brush the top with vinaigrette, and cook for 3 to 4 minutes. Flip again and brush the top with vinaigrette.

SERVE IT UP on lightly toasted hamburger buns

TOP IT OFF with red leaf lettuce and thinly sliced tomato

ASIAN TUNA BURGERS WITH WASABI MAYO

MAKES 6 BURGERS

East meets West in one of our all-time favorites. Rich with ginger and scallions, this burger's Asian flavors boast extra smokiness and depth that only a good old barbecue can give. The Wasabi Mayo totally rocks with this burger, but if Japanese horseradish makes you cry, cut down on the wasabi. FYI: Wasabi is one of the hardest-to-grow vegetables in the world, so most of what's available is actually a mixture of regular horseradish, mustard, and food coloring.

1½ pounds tuna steaks

2 cloves garlic, minced

2 teaspoons peeled and minced fresh ginger

1 tablespoon toasted sesame oil

3 tablespoons soy sauce

¼ cup chopped scallions (white and green parts)

½ teaspoon salt

¼ teaspoon coarsely ground black pepper

1. Cut half the tuna into ¼-inch dice and mince the other half. Combine the tuna, garlic, ginger, sesame oil, soy sauce, scallions, salt, and pepper in a large mixing bowl. Form into 6 patties, each 1 inch thick.
2. Lightly oil the grill or a skillet over medium-high heat and cook the burgers until browned on both sides and to the desired degree of doneness (the middle can still be reddish pink), 5 to 7 minutes total.

SERVE IT UP on toasted sesame seed buns

TOP IT OFF with Wasabi Mayo (recipe follows)

Wasabi Mayo

MAKES ABOUT ½ CUP

Don't be fooled by the tame color. Its spicy zing will wake up burgers and other sandwiches.

¼ cup plus 2 tablespoons mayonnaise

3 tablespoons minced scallions (white and green parts)

2 teaspoons peeled and minced fresh ginger

2 teaspoons soy sauce

1 teaspoon wasabi paste or powder

Process all the ingredients together in a food processor until smooth. Taste and adjust the seasonings. This will keep, tightly covered, in the refrigerator for up to 1 week.

NUDE DUKE INVENTS MAYO

It's ironic that mayonnaise might have been invented by a man who liked to dress his food but not himself. The duc de Richelieu is thought to have invented mayo in 1756, after he conquered the Spanish island of Minorca. The French duke was a flamboyant party animal who reportedly liked to entertain his dinner guests in the nude.

TUNA SHISO BURGERS WITH ASIAN SALSA

MAKES 4 BURGERS

You may know Emmy-winning chef Ming Tsai as the affable host of the Food Network's popular cooking show *East Meets West with Ming Tsai*. He's also the chef/owner of Blue Ginger, an Asian fusion restaurant in Wellesley, Massachusetts, that Jane couldn't stop talking about. This tuna burger—courtesy of Ming and sous chef Terrence Maul—is rich and scrumptious, and perfectly reflects Ming's Chinese heritage and European training.

1 ¼ pounds center-cut tuna, any dark spots trimmed away

¼ cup (½ stick) cold unsalted butter

8 large fresh shiso (see Ingredient Glossary, page 227) or basil leaves, chopped

2 scallions (white and green parts), thinly sliced

1 tablespoon soy sauce

Salt and coarsely ground black pepper to taste

1. Using a meat grinder or food processor, grind the tuna and butter together so that the butter is in very small pieces. Fold in the shiso, scallions, and soy sauce, then season with salt and pepper. Form the mixture into 4 patties, each about 1 inch thick.
2. Prepare an outdoor grill, preheat the broiler, or heat a skillet over medium-high heat and cook the burgers to the desired degree of doneness, 6 to 8 minutes per side for medium rare.

SERVE IT UP on hamburger buns

TOP IT OFF with red leaf lettuce and Asian Salsa (recipe follows)

Asian Salsa

MAKES ABOUT 1¼ CUPS

For a Mexican twist, serve any extra in a bowl with tortilla chips.

2 small, ripe tomatoes, cut into ¼-inch dice (about ½ cup)

½ small red onion, diced

¼ bunch fresh cilantro leaves, finely chopped (about ¼ cup)

1 clove garlic, finely chopped

Juice of 2 limes

1 tablespoon extra virgin olive oil

Salt and coarsely ground black pepper to taste

In a medium-size nonreactive bowl, combine the tomatoes, onion, cilantro, and garlic. Add the lime juice and oil and season with salt and pepper. Let the mixture sit for 30 minutes to allow the flavors to develop.

SACRAMENTO'S BURGER GUYS BOOST HOMETOWN FAVORITE

Sacramento's Burger Guys (www.fcusd.k12.ca.us/chsweb/burgers/burgerindex.htm) are so burger obsessed that they observed, "It is not a coincidence that the Cold War ended three days after Jack-in-the-Box and Burger King opened franchises two blocks from the Kremlin." Whatever! They review burger joints in other states but swear that Ford's Real Hamburgers in their hometown is the "gold standard"—something to do with the paprika that Ford sprinkles on its patties.

Ford's Real Hamburgers • 1948 Sutterville Road • Sacramento, CA 95822 • (916) 452-6979

CONCH BURGERS

MAKES 4 BURGERS

Once upon a time, queen conchs were as plentiful as palm trees in the Florida Keys. Highly prized for its beautiful pink spiral shell and sweet succulent meat, the queen conch is now on the commercially threatened list due to overfishing. So the conch we get in the States is imported mostly from the Caribbean. If you can't find queen conch, scungilli—a type of whelk found in Italian markets—is an acceptable substitute.

1 pound conch meat (see Ingredient Sources, page 230), cut into ½-inch dice

1 tablespoon fresh lemon juice

1 medium-size onion, finely chopped

2 cloves garlic, minced

½ cup seeded and finely chopped red bell pepper

2 teaspoons ground allspice

2 teaspoons dried thyme

1 teaspoon salt

½ teaspoon cayenne pepper

½ teaspoon coarsely ground black pepper

½ teaspoon paprika

1 teaspoon Tabasco sauce

1 teaspoon Worcestershire sauce

1 cup plain dry bread crumbs

3 tablespoons canola oil

1. In a food processor, grind together the conch, lemon juice, onion, garlic, and bell pepper. Add the allspice, thyme, salt, cayenne, black pepper, paprika, Tabasco, and Worcestershire and pulse until

combined. Scrape the mixture into a medium-size mixing bowl. Add the bread crumbs and mix well. Form into 4 patties, each ½ inch thick.

2. Heat the oil in a medium-size skillet over high heat and cook the burgers until golden brown, 3 to 5 minutes per side.

SERVE IT UP on toasted garlic bread, egg bread, or challah

TOP IT OFF with Mango Salsa (page 163) or Red Pepper Mayo (page 67)

WHERE THE FAMOUS CHOW DOWN IN THE CONCH REPUBLIC

Legend has it that John Glenn ate here after his first flight into space. This pharmacy/luncheonette/one-hour photo lab is where Conchs (Key West natives) come for their morning coffee. Later in the day, just about everybody comes here for Cuban food or all-American burgers. Jimmy Buffett, the composer of "Cheeseburger in Paradise," is said to have eaten many a burger at the counter.

Conch Cupboard Luncheonette • 1229 Simonton Street, in Dennis Pharmacy
Key West, FL 33040 • (305) 294-1577

JALAPEÑO CRAB BURGERS WITH MANGO SALSA

MAKES 6 BURGERS

If you love spicy food, you'll find these crab burgers irresistible. The jalapeño plays up the crabmeat's natural sweetness. The tropical heat of the Mango Salsa is also excellent over grilled fish. Be sure to pick through the crabmeat to remove any leftover cartilage or shells.

1 pound jumbo lump crabmeat, picked over for shells and cartilage

¼ cup mayonnaise

2 tablespoons Worcestershire sauce

½ teaspoon cayenne pepper

1 fresh jalapeño chile pepper, seeded and finely chopped

3 tablespoons minced shallots

¼ teaspoon coarsely ground black pepper

Pinch of salt

2 tablespoons fresh lemon juice

⅓ cup plus 2 tablespoons plain dry bread crumbs

2 tablespoons vegetable oil

1. Preheat the oven to 375°F.
2. Mix together the crabmeat, mayonnaise, Worcestershire, cayenne, jalapeño, shallots, black pepper, salt, lemon juice, and 2 tablespoons of the bread crumbs in a large mixing bowl.
3. To make the burgers, pack one-sixth of the mixture into a ½-cup measure and place the patty on a baking sheet. Repeat with the remaining mixture. Spread the remaining ⅓ cup bread crumbs on waxed paper and gently press the burgers into them, turning to coat evenly.

4. In a medium-size nonstick skillet, heat 1 tablespoon of the vegetable oil over medium-high heat. Gently add 3 of the burgers and pan-fry until golden brown, 3 to 5 minutes. Turn the burgers carefully and brown the other side. Transfer the burgers to a baking sheet. Repeat with the remaining 3 burgers.
5. Place the crab burgers in the oven and bake until heated through, 5 to 7 minutes.

SERVE IT UP on warm soft rolls

TOP IT OFF with Mango Salsa (recipe follows)

Mango Salsa

MAKES 1 CUP

For some real tropical heat, add about one-quarter teaspoon of diced Scotch bonnet chile pepper.

2 ripe mangoes (about 1 pound each), peeled, seeded, and cut into ¼-inch dice

½ cup red onion cut into ¼-inch dice

2 tablespoons chopped fresh cilantro leaves

2 teaspoons red wine vinegar

2 teaspoons sugar (optional)

¼ teaspoon salt

¼ teaspoon red pepper flakes

Combine all the ingredients in a medium-size bowl until well blended. Serve at room temperature.

CARIBBEAN CRAB BURGERS WITH PAPAYA CHUTNEY

MAKES 4 BURGERS

Visions of rum punch and sugar white beaches may leap to mind when you taste these spicy crab burgers. First you make a *sofrito*, a Spanish flavor base usually containing lard, onions, green peppers, and annatto, a natural food coloring. Our version contains no lard but is still packed with flavor.

3 tablespoons olive oil

½ cup seeded and finely chopped green bell pepper

½ medium-size yellow onion, finely chopped

2 scallions (white and green parts), minced

1 pound jumbo lump crabmeat, picked over for shells and cartilage

1 clove garlic, minced

1 large egg

3 tablespoons plain dry bread crumbs

2 tablespoons minced fresh cilantro leaves

1 tablespoon fresh lemon juice

1 teaspoon paprika

½ teaspoon ground cumin

½ teaspoon dried oregano

½ teaspoon salt

½ teaspoon coarsely ground black pepper

1. To make the *sofrito*, heat 1 tablespoon of the oil in a large skillet over medium-high heat. Add the bell pepper, onion, and scallions and cook, stirring, until just softened, about 2 minutes. Let cool.

2. In a medium-size mixing bowl, gently mix together the crabmeat, garlic, egg, bread crumbs, cilantro, lemon juice, paprika, cumin, oregano, salt, pepper, and *sofrito*. Form into 4 patties, each 1 inch thick.
3. Heat the remaining 2 tablespoons oil in a large skillet over medium-high heat. Add the burgers and cook until golden brown, 3 to 4 minutes per side. Drain on paper towels and serve immediately.

SERVE IT UP on toasted buttered garlic bread

TOP IT OFF with Papaya Chutney (recipe follows)

Papaya Chutney

MAKES 3 CUPS

Try pineapple instead of papaya for another tropical take.

2 tablespoons canola oil

1 cup seeded and chopped red bell pepper

½ medium-size red onion, finely chopped

½ teaspoon cayenne pepper

½ cup orange juice

¼ cup apple juice

¾ cup cider vinegar

½ cup firmly packed light brown sugar

4 cups peeled, seeded, and diced ripe papaya

1. Heat the oil in a medium-size saucepan over medium-high heat. Add the bell pepper and onion and cook, stirring, until just softened, 4 to 6 minutes. Add the cayenne, orange juice, apple juice, vinegar, and brown sugar. Bring to a boil, reduce the heat to low, and simmer until thickened, about 15 minutes.
2. Add the papaya and cook until soft and pulpy, about 20 minutes. Taste and adjust the seasonings and let cool. This will keep, tightly covered, in the refrigerator for up to 3 days.

LAURIE'S DUNGENESS CRAB BURGERS WITH SWEET ROASTED PEPPER ROUILLE

MAKES 8 BURGERS, OR 4 SERVINGS

Chef Laurie Paul and her partner, Tim Barrette, garnered critical praise from *Bon Appétit* and *Gourmet* magazines for their honest, seasonal cooking and use of regional ingredients at the Friday Harbor House in Washington State. These crab cakes are a signature dish from Laurie, who has recently opened a gourmet food store. Stop by the Market Chef if you are ever in Friday Harbor, in the San Juan Islands. Tell them we sent you.

1 pound fresh Dungeness crabmeat or jumbo lump crabmeat, picked over for shells and cartilage

⅓ cup Sweet Roasted Pepper Rouille (page 168)

1 cup fresh bread crumbs

⅓ cup pecans, toasted (see Note, page 143) and finely chopped

¼ cup chopped onion

3 tablespoons seeded and chopped red bell pepper

3 tablespoons seeded and chopped yellow bell pepper

1 stalk celery, chopped

1 large egg

Salt and freshly ground black pepper to taste

1½ tablespoons corn oil

1. Preheat the oven to 425°F.
2. In a large mixing bowl, combine the crabmeat, rouille, bread crumbs, pecans, onion, bell peppers, and celery, mixing gently with a large rubber spatula. Beat the egg with healthy pinches of salt and black

pepper. Add the beaten egg mixture and corn oil to the crab mixture and mix thoroughly, adding more salt and pepper to taste.

3. Form the mixture into 8 patties, each ¾ inch thick, using either your hands or a 4-ounce ice cream scoop. Place the cakes on a greased baking sheet and bake until golden, about 12 minutes.

SERVE IT UP on fresh rolls

TOP IT OFF with more of the rouille

Sweet Roasted Pepper Rouille

MAKES 2 TO 2½ CUPS

Pair this with Dilled Chickpea Burgers (page 206) for another intriguing combo.

1 medium-size red or yellow bell pepper

Juice of 2 lemons

1 tablespoon white wine vinegar

1½ tablespoons capers, with their brine

3 large egg yolks

1 large egg

1 tablespoon chopped garlic

¼ cup fresh bread crumbs

1 teaspoon cayenne pepper

1 teaspoon ground cinnamon

2 teaspoons sugar

3 teaspoons salt, or more to taste

2 cups corn oil

¼ to ½ cup water, as needed

1. Roast the bell pepper over an open flame or under the broiler, turning until the skin is charred on all sides. Place in a small bowl, cover with plastic wrap, and let sit until cool enough to handle. Remove the skin, seeds, and white ribs.
2. In a food processor, combine the roasted pepper, lemon juice, vinegar, capers, egg yolks, egg, garlic, bread crumbs, cayenne, cinnamon, sugar, and salt and process into a loose paste. With the motor running, add the corn oil through the feed tube in a slow, steady stream until the mixture thickens. Add enough of the water to thin the sauce to a mayonnaise-like consistency. Refrigerate for 30 minutes to thicken before serving.

CRAWFISH PORK BURGERS WITH SCALLION MAYONNAISE

MAKES 4 BURGERS

Bring the Big Easy to your kitchen with this crawfish burger by New Orleans restaurateur Susan Spicer. Crawfish, or crayfish, is a tiny crustacean well loved by Cajuns. It looks like a pocket-size lobster but is, in fact, no relation. Spicer is the award-winning owner and chef of Bayona, a French Quarter epicure's delight housed in a 200-year-old Creole cottage. She generously shared this sophisticated yet easy-to-prepare hybrid burger recipe with us. The shellfish and pork combo mixes it up like a memorable jazz riff that hits just the right notes.

½ pound ground pork (we also tried ground dark meat turkey—delicious!)

1 pound crawfish tails (available frozen in many supermarkets or see Ingredient Sources, page 230, for fresh) or shrimp, peeled, deveined, and roughly chopped

1 large egg white, lightly beaten

½ medium-size onion, finely chopped

¼ cup seeded and finely chopped red bell pepper

1 teaspoon minced garlic

1 teaspoon chopped fresh thyme leaves

1 tablespoon chopped fresh flat-leaf parsley leaves

Pinch of red pepper flakes

Pinch of salt

1. In a large mixing bowl, combine all the ingredients. Pinch off a piece of the mixture and sauté it to check the seasoning. Form into 4 patties, each 1 inch thick.

2. Lightly oil the grill or a large skillet over medium-high heat. Reduce the heat to medium, add the burgers, and cook until a light brown crust forms, 3 to 5 minutes. Flip the burgers and cook for 5 minutes more.

SERVE IT UP on toasted French bread

TOP IT OFF with pepper Jack cheese and Scallion Mayonnaise (recipe follows)

BURGERS UNDER HUBCAPS?

Is all that jambalaya and crawfish étouffée getting to you? If so, head over to Poppy's Grill for a beef burger. This ain't no humble diner—it boasts the "Earth's Best Burgers," with a beef patty that's fried under a hubcap to seal in the juices. Or try Poppy's special bacon-mushroom cheeseburger, a New Orleans favorite that you can top off with a fried egg.

Poppy's Grill • 717 St. Peter Street • New Orleans, LA 70116 • (504) 524-3287

www.poppysgrill.com

Scallion Mayonnaise

MAKES ABOUT 1¼ CUPS

Leave out the lime juice if you want a mellower flavor.

1 bunch scallions (about 6)

1 cup plus 1 tablespoon olive oil

Juice of 1 lime

Salt and coarsely ground black pepper to taste

2 large egg yolks

1 teaspoon Dijon mustard

1 teaspoon red wine vinegar

1. Trim the tops and bottoms of the scallions. Place in a glass baking dish, coat with 1 tablespoon of the olive oil and half of the lime juice, and season with salt and pepper. Grill lightly or sauté just until limp, 2 to 4 minutes. Remove from the heat and let cool, then roughly chop.
2. Place the egg yolks, mustard, vinegar, and scallions in a food processor and pulse until just combined. With the machine running, add the remaining 1 cup oil through the feed tube in a slow, steady stream until thickened. Season with salt and pepper and stir in the remaining lime juice. Keep refrigerated until ready to serve. It will keep, tightly covered, in the refrigerator for several days.

LOBSTER BURGERS WITH HEARTS OF PALM AND SAUCE VERTE

MAKES 6 BURGERS

Talk about delicious! Sweet chunks of lobster are paired with hearts of palm and carrots for added tanginess and texture. The green sauce gives just the right touch of creamy sharpness. This is an expensive and elegant burger—reserve it for special guests or a romantic summertime meal.

1 pound cooked lobster meat, finely chopped

½ cup hearts of palm, drained and finely chopped

2 tablespoons finely chopped fresh chives

3 tablespoons olive oil

½ cup finely chopped leeks (white and green parts)

½ cup finely diced carrot

½ teaspoon salt

¼ teaspoon coarsely ground black pepper

1 cup cooked Great Northern or other white beans, rinsed and well drained

1 large egg

½ cup panko (see Ingredient Sources, page 232) or plain dry bread crumbs

1. Combine the lobster, hearts of palm, and chives in a large mixing bowl. Set aside.
2. Heat 1 tablespoon of the olive oil in a small skillet over medium heat. Add the leeks and carrot, and cook, stirring, until barely softened, 2 to 4 minutes. Transfer to the bowl with the lobster. Add the salt and pepper and mix.
3. Place the beans and egg in a food processor or blender and process until smooth. Add to the lobster mixture and mix well. Add the panko and combine gently. Form into 6 patties, each 1 inch thick.

4. Heat 1 tablespoon of the olive oil in a large skillet over medium heat. Add 3 of the patties and pan-fry until a nice crispy crust forms, 3 to 4 minutes. Turn and cook the other side until crispy, 3 to 4 minutes. Transfer the patties to a platter and keep warm. Repeat with the remaining 3 patties.

SERVE IT UP on brioche bread or rolls

TOP IT OFF with Sauce Verte (recipe follows)

Sauce Verte

MAKES ABOUT 3/4 CUP

The brilliant green color of this sauce also looks and tastes great with the coral pink of Shelley's Salmon Croquette Burgers (page 145).

4 scallions (white and green parts), chopped

½ cup capers, drained

1 cup chopped fresh cilantro leaves

½ teaspoon salt

2 tablespoons Dijon mustard

1 tablespoon olive oil

Process all the ingredients together in a food processor until creamy.

WOO YOU OYSTER BURGERS

MAKES 4 BURGERS

It's no secret that the oyster is considered an aphrodisiac. We're not sure of its ability to seduce, but we think that you'll fall in love with this burger once you've had it. Make sure you get fresh, plump oysters. Their liquor should be clear, not milky. Forget the old myth about avoiding oysters in months that don't have the letter *r*. These days, quick transport and refrigeration make oysters available year-round.

1 pint fresh oysters, drained and chopped

1 cup seasoned dry bread crumbs

⅓ cup finely grated onion

Generous pinch of cayenne pepper

¼ teaspoon salt

1 teaspoon Worcestershire sauce

2 teaspoons fresh lemon juice

¼ cup mayonnaise

2 tablespoons chopped fresh chives

1 tablespoon canola oil

1 tablespoon unsalted butter

1. In a medium-size mixing bowl, gently combine all the ingredients except the oil and butter. Form into 4 patties, each about 1 inch thick.
2. In a large skillet, heat the oil and butter together over medium heat until the butter melts and cook the burgers until golden brown, 3 to 4 minutes per side.

SERVE IT UP on French bread or Nancy Silverton's Hamburger Buns (page 49)

TOP IT OFF with cocktail sauce, mayonnaise, or both

ALL GUNSMOKE AND BURGERS

Sounds like the Buck Snort Saloon is a place for atmosphere as well as burgers. According to Lori Midson of Denver's Digital City Web site, everyone from "leather-clad bikers" to "hip-hugging trendsetters" make the trek to this rustic log cabin saloon. We hear the 8-ounce Buck Burger alone is worth the trip.

Buck Snort Saloon • 15921 Elk Creek Road • Pine, CO 80470 • (303) 838-0284

SCALLOP BURGERS
WITH CELERIAC AND SPICY MAYO

MAKES 4 BURGERS

We think scallops are the creamiest, most succulent shellfish to emerge from the ocean. This burger makes the most of their briny sweetness, while the celeriac adds a subtle licorice flavor. Celeriac is also called celery root and is a member of the umbel family, which also includes fennel and parsley.

1 tablespoon plus 1 teaspoon olive oil
½ cup peeled celeriac cut into ¼-inch dice
2 tablespoons mayonnaise (preferably homemade)
1 teaspoon Dijon mustard
½ teaspoon Worcestershire sauce
1 pound sea scallops, finely chopped
1 tablespoon finely chopped fresh chives
1 large egg, lightly beaten
1 cup panko (see Ingredient Sources, page 232) or plain dry bread crumbs

1. Heat 1 teaspoon of the olive oil in a small skillet over medium heat. Add the celeriac and cook, stirring, until just softened, 3 to 4 minutes. Remove from the heat.
2. In a small bowl, mix together the mayonnaise, mustard, and Worcestershire.
3. Combine the scallops, celeriac, mayonnaise mixture, chives, egg, and panko in a large mixing bowl. Form into 4 patties, each ¾ inch thick.
4. Heat the remaining 1 tablespoon olive oil in a large skillet over medium heat. Add the burgers and pan-fry until slightly crispy on one side, 2 to 4 minutes. Turn and cook the other side for 2 to 4 minutes.

SERVE IT UP on egg bread or challah

TOP IT OFF with extra Dijon mustard or Sauce Verte (page 173)

AN OCEAN OF PROTEIN

Global fish production exceeds that of cattle, sheep, poultry, or eggs. Fish are the largest source of protein in the world.

SCALLOP AND COD QUENELLE BURGERS WITH VELOUTÉ SAUCE

MAKES 8 SERVINGS

This recipe is a refined riff on the burger. It's based on a *quenelle*, a French-style dumpling that's poached in a liquid and served with a white sauce—kind of like a dressed-up gefilte fish. Classic *quenelles* are rich in flavor and calories. We've lightened ours, using milk instead of cream and cutting down on the butter, but we just couldn't resist the traditional creamy sauce. Salmon would work in place of the cod. We top it off with a little Parmesan, but you can opt for horseradish instead and call it a gefilte *quenelle*.

1 pound sea scallops, cut into small chunks

1 pound cod fillets, any bones removed and cut into small chunks

1 large egg

2 large egg whites

1 cup whole milk

½ teaspoon salt

¼ teaspoon coarsely ground black pepper

2 tablespoons chopped fresh dill

1 tablespoon chopped fresh savory leaves

1 tablespoon chopped fresh chives

1 tablespoon unsalted butter

1 tablespoon all-purpose flour

½ cup minced shallots

2 cups white wine

3 tablespoons freshly grated Parmesan cheese, for serving

1. Preheat the broiler. In a food processor, process the scallops and cod together into a coarse paste. Add the egg, egg whites, milk, salt, pepper, 1 tablespoon of the dill, the savory, and chives and process until well combined. Transfer the mixture to a large mixing bowl and refrigerate.
2. In a small bowl, knead the butter and flour together until they form a paste. Set aside.
3. In a large skillet over medium-high heat, combine the shallots, the remaining 1 tablespoon dill, and the wine and bring to a simmer.
4. Using 2 large serving spoons, form the fish mixture into oblong patties and gently drop them into the poaching liquid. Reduce the heat to medium and simmer for 5 minutes. Gently flip with a slotted spoon and cook until opaque all the way through, 3 to 5 minutes more. Using the spoon, transfer to a baking sheet. Repeat until you've cooked all the patties.
5. Reduce the heat to medium-low and slowly add bits of the butter-flour paste until the sauce thickens and the flour mixture is cooked through, 3 to 5 minutes.

SERVE IT UP Place 2 *quenelles* on the bottom of a toasted French roll or brioche roll, spoon some of the pan sauce on the *quenelles*, top with some Parmesan, and broil until slightly browned, 1 to 2 minutes.

TOP IT OFF with more pan sauce, fresh or pan-fried baby spinach leaves, and prepared horseradish

IT TAKE ALL KINDS

There are literally hundreds of varieties of mustard, from fancy Dijon to the classic ballpark favorite. This bright yellow version was first made by George French (as in French's mustard), who used turmeric to create its trademark golden color.

SHRIMP AND EGGPLANT BURGERS WITH ORANGE SNOW PEA SALAD

MAKES 6 BURGERS

Europeans call it *aubergine*. We call it eggplant. But what's in a name? Either way, it's delicious when paired with shrimp. The secret ingredient of this rich fish cake is hoisin sauce, a sweet and spicy Chinese condiment. Be sure to cut the eggplant and shrimp into very small pieces so the patties hold together.

1 small eggplant

3 tablespoons plus 1 teaspoon olive oil

Juice of ½ lemon

½ cup finely chopped scallions (green part only)

Salt and coarsely ground black pepper to taste

1 pound shrimp, peeled, deveined, and minced

2 tablespoons hoisin sauce

½ cup plain dry bread crumbs

1. Peel the eggplant and cut into very small dice or coarsely grind in a food processor. You need about 3 cups.
2. Heat 2 tablespoons of the olive oil in large skillet over medium heat, add the eggplant and cook, stirring, until it cooks down, about 10 minutes. Add the lemon juice and scallions and continue to cook until the eggplant is soft and pulpy and all the moisture has evaporated, about 10 minutes. Season with salt and pepper and transfer to a large mixing bowl.
3. Add the shrimp and hoisin and combine well. Gently form into 6 patties, each about 1 inch thick. Coat the patties evenly on all sides with the bread crumbs.

4. In a large skillet over medium heat, heat 2 teaspoons of the olive oil. Add 3 of the burgers, turn gently after 6 to 8 minutes, and cook for 6 minutes more, until heated through. Repeat with the remaining 3 burgers.

SERVE IT UP in warm pita pockets

TOP IT OFF with Orange Snow Pea Salad (recipe follows)

Orange Snow Pea Salad

MAKES 4 CUPS

A little citrus and a lot of crunch, with an Asian accent.

2 navel oranges

½ pound snow peas, quartered widthwise

2 tablespoons soy sauce

2 tablespoons olive oil

1½ teaspoons white or black sesame seeds, or a mixture, toasted (see Note)

1. Use a wide vegetable peeler to remove the zest of half of 1 orange in long strips. Cut the strips into 2-inch-long matchsticks.
2. Use a knife to remove the rind and white pith from the oranges. Cut the oranges into small segments over a bowl, reserving the juice. Place the orange pieces in a large serving bowl, then add the snow peas and zest.
3. In a small bowl, whisk together the soy sauce, 2 tablespoons of the reserved orange juice, and the olive oil. Add to the salad, sprinkle with the sesame seeds, and toss well to combine. Serve immediately.

NOTE **To toast sesame seeds, place them in a small skillet over medium-low heat and toast, shaking the pan gently, until fragrant, about 2 minutes. Be careful not to let them burn.**

SHRIMP GUMBO BURGERS

MAKES 4 BURGERS

This recipe was obviously inspired by the popular Creole dish. What you don't know is that it's way spicy, with three kinds of pepper: cayenne, black, and white. The legendary New Orleans chef Paul Prudhomme points out that each pepper acts differently on your palate, hitting you in a timed sequence, like a fireworks display.

2 tablespoons olive oil

1 cup finely chopped okra

⅓ cup finely chopped scallions (white and green parts)

¼ teaspoon cayenne pepper

¼ teaspoon coarsely ground black pepper

¼ teaspoon ground white pepper

1 teaspoon crushed dried thyme

1 pound shrimp, peeled, deveined, and finely chopped

½ cup cooked white rice

½ medium-size yellow onion, finely chopped

½ cup seeded and finely diced green bell pepper

½ cup finely chopped celery

2 cloves garlic, minced

1 cup quartered cherry or grape tomatoes

½ teaspoon salt

¼ cup chopped fresh flat-leaf parsley leaves

¾ cup fish broth or clam juice

1 tablespoon tomato paste

1. Heat 1 tablespoon of the oil in a large skillet over medium-high heat. Add the okra; scallions; ⅛ teaspoon each of the cayenne, black pepper, and white pepper; and ½ teaspoon of the thyme. Reduce the heat to medium and cook, stirring, for 3 to 5 minutes. Remove from the heat.
2. In a large mixing bowl, combine the okra mixture, shrimp, and rice. Form into 4 patties, each ¾ inch thick, cover with plastic wrap, and refrigerate for at least 30 minutes to firm up.
3. Using the same skillet, heat the remaining 1 tablespoon oil over medium-high heat. Add the onion, bell pepper, celery, and garlic and cook, stirring frequently, until just softened, 2 to 4 minutes. Add the tomatoes; the remaining ⅛ teaspoon each cayenne, black pepper, and white pepper; the remaining ½ teaspoon thyme; the salt; parsley; broth; and tomato paste. Reduce the heat to medium-low and cook, stirring, for 3 to 5 minutes.
4. Add the patties to the pan and simmer in the sauce for 10 minutes on each side.

SERVE IT UP on lightly toasted French baguettes or toasted English muffins

TOP IT OFF with the gumbo mixture

GETTING DRESSED IN NEW ORLEANS

In the "Big Easy," a sandwich is "dressed" when it's served with lettuce, tomato, and mayonnaise.

SHRIMP AND FENNEL BURGERS

MAKES 6 BURGERS

Prepare these confetti-flecked patties ahead of time. Their sophisticated flavor, pleasing texture, and attractive presentation will have your friends thinking you slaved away for hours. The fact is, they cook up quickly, just before serving. So relax with your guests—all you need is 10 to 15 minutes to cook them. Of course, company can always join you in the kitchen and dress the finished patties with the bright green sauce while you pour the wine.

¼ cup olive oil

1 cup finely chopped leeks (white part only)

1 cup finely chopped fennel bulb

½ cup seeded and finely diced fresh jalapeño chile peppers

½ cup finely chopped carrot

1 pound shrimp, peeled, deveined, and finely chopped

1 tablespoon Dijon mustard

1 large egg

1. Heat 2 tablespoons of the oil in a large skillet over medium-high heat. Add the leeks, fennel, jalapeños, and carrot and cook over medium heat, stirring frequently, until softened, 3 to 5 minutes.
2. In a large mixing bowl, combine the sautéed vegetables, shrimp, mustard, and egg. To make the burgers, pack one-sixth of the mixture into a ½-cup measure and place the patty on a baking sheet. Repeat with the remaining mixture. Cover with plastic wrap and refrigerate for at least 30 minutes.
3. Heat 1 tablespoon of the oil in a skillet over medium heat. Add 3 burgers and cook until a crust forms, about 5 minutes. Flip and cook through, 5 to 7 minutes more. Repeat with remaining burgers.

SERVE IT UP on lightly toasted sourdough bread or Nancy Silverton's Hamburger Buns (page 49)

TOP IT OFF with Sauce Verte (page 173) or Roasted Yellow Pepper Sauce (page 141)

THAI SHRIMP AND CRAB BURGERS

MAKES 4 BURGERS

Thai red curry paste is the dominant flavor in these burgers, which cook up to be a rich orange hue. The paste, made from chile peppers, garlic, and various other spices, packs a wallop, so you need only a little. If you can't find fish sauce, use soy sauce. But the red curry paste is a must.

½ pound medium-size shrimp, peeled and deveined

1 large egg

¼ cup water

1 cup plain dry bread crumbs

2 tablespoons Thai red curry paste (see Ingredient Sources, page 232)

1½ tablespoons minced fresh cilantro leaves

2 teaspoons peeled and minced fresh ginger

2 tablespoons minced shallots

1½ tablespoons fish sauce (available in Asian markets)

6 ounces jumbo lump crabmeat, picked over for shells and cartilage

1. In a food processor, pulse the shrimp until it resembles a coarse paste. Add the egg, water, and bread crumbs and pulse again. Transfer the mixture to a medium-size mixing bowl. Add the curry paste, cilantro, ginger, shallots, and fish sauce and mix well. Gently fold in the crabmeat, taking care not to break up too many of the lumps. Form into 4 patties, each ¾ inch thick.
2. Lightly oil the grill or a skillet over high heat and cook the burgers just until opaque all the way through, 1 to 2 minutes per side.

SERVE IT UP wrapped in lavash

TOP IT OFF with Spicy Cucumber Salad (page 113)

Juicy Portobello Burgers and Mesclun in Pita Pockets ◌ Grilled Portobello and Spinach Burgers ◌ Mushroom Goat Cheese Burgers with Sun-Dried Tomato Chutney ◌

Veggie Burgers:

Cauliflower Cremini Burgers with Orange Basil Sauce ◌ Eggplant Parmigiana Burgers ◌ Brussels Sprout, Apple, and Walnut Burgers ◌ Jalapeño, Artichoke, and Corn Burgers with Cilantro Cream Sauce ◌ Asian Salad Burgers ◌ Dilled Chickpea

Redefining the Burger

For too long, vegetables were shoved to the back of the culinary burner—especially when it came to burgers. But veggies are finally getting their day in the sun, as people discover them to be a sensual, delicious smorgasbord of versatile ingredients. No other food group offers such complex possibilities of flavors, textures, colors, and shapes.

Whether offering plump, juicy tomatoes or sweet, fresh corn, farmers' markets are brimming with produce at its peak. And many supermarkets offer a range of ethnic vegetables and herbs that was virtually unheard-of even five years ago.

Lean Greens

Healthy eating and better produce may be two reasons that veggie burgers are gaining in popularity. The Gardenburger brand alone has reportedly sold more than 500 million patties and expects to sell its billionth veggie burger in 2003.

Choose your veggie, then throw in some chopped nuts, perhaps some rice, a splash of wine—and you've got the makings of a veggie burger. Unleash your creativity. Mix in nuts, grains, even pasta for added texture.

But watch out! Green isn't lean if you add a lot of saturated fat, which means keep an eye on creamy dressings, mayonnaise, and high-fat cheeses.

Listen to Your Mom

She was right: eat your veggies, because they are loaded with nutrients. You won't find a better source for beta carotene, fiber, folic acid, vitamin C, and vitamin A. Veggies have heart-healthy benefits and can help prevent cancer. In fact, scientists are looking increasingly to vegetables as a source of all sorts of health advantages.

The USDA recommends three to five servings of veggies a day. Veggie burgers are a great way to satisfy this daily allowance while satisfying your appetite as well.

The ABCs of Veggie Burgers

The hardest part about making veggie burgers is holding them together. Recipes that use starchy vegetables hold their shape very well, but other, more delicate veggie patties need careful handling. Here are some suggestions.

- Binders are key to holding veggie burgers together. Legumes such as chickpeas and black beans are ideal. Other options are eggs (if you want to forgo the fat, substitute two egg whites for one whole egg) and bread crumbs (we especially like panko, Japanese bread crumbs, which are lighter in texture than regular crumbs).
- Cut your ingredients into small pieces to ensure that your burgers hold their shape.
- In the recipes that call for tofu, drain the tofu very well, squeezing out as much liquid as you can. Otherwise, your burgers will be likely to fall apart.
- Refrigerate your uncooked patties for 30 minutes or more to firm them up. We indicate this in the recipes where it is critical. It's not necessary for the other recipes, but it does offer some insurance that they will hold together nicely during cooking.
- Cook your veggie burgers in a skillet, which also will help them hold their shape.

The key to good, fresh vegetables is seasonality. That means to get the absolutely best quality, try to buy locally grown vegetables in season—such as corn in summer, pumpkins in fall, Brussels sprouts in winter, and sweet peas in spring. Veggie burgers also make great side dishes, but we think they can stand on their own.

JUICY PORTOBELLO BURGERS AND MESCLUN IN PITA POCKETS

MAKES 4 BURGERS

These earthy mushrooms are first bathed in a Mediterranean-style marinade of garlic, lemon juice, and olive oil. The mixture softens the mushrooms' dense texture and infuses them with a heady flavor and aroma.

- **8 medium-size portobello mushrooms, stems removed**
- **½ cup olive oil**
- **3 large cloves garlic, minced**
- **½ cup fresh lemon juice**
- **¼ teaspoon salt**
- **Mesclun salad mix tossed with Sherry Wine Vinaigrette (recipe follows), for topping**

1. Place the mushroom caps upside down on a baking sheet.
2. Whisk together the olive oil, garlic, lemon juice, and salt and pour it evenly over the mushrooms. Make sure the marinade pools up in the undersides of the mushrooms. Turn them a few times during their bath so that both sides get liberally coated. Marinate for at least 30 minutes.
3. Lightly oil the grill or a skillet over medium-high heat and cook the mushrooms for about 5 minutes per side, longer if you want a slightly crispy crust.

SERVE IT UP by placing 2 mushrooms in a warm pita pocket or wrap in warm lavash

TOP IT OFF with the mesclun

Sherry Wine Vinaigrette

MAKES 2 TABLESPOONS

2 tablespoons extra virgin olive oil

¼ teaspoon sherry wine vinegar

¼ teaspoon salt

Mix everything together in a cup.

A PHILADELPHIA STORY

Loyal customers flock to Fergie's in Philly's Center City for its thick Fergie Burger, topped with mounds of sautéed onions, mushrooms, and provolone cheese. Another popular burger is the Kipper, with bacon, American cheese, and mayo. For vegetarians, there's the Black Bean and Portabella Burger. One great bonus: Fergie's spicy fries, which come with every burger.

Fergie's Pub • 1214 Sansom Street • Philadelphia, PA 19107 • (215) 928-8118

www.fergies.com

GRILLED PORTOBELLO AND SPINACH BURGERS

MAKES 4 BURGERS

Rich and meaty, the portobello is known as the steak of mushrooms. Despite its sexy name, it is just a regular brown cremini mushroom all grown up. In fact, it is the largest and hardiest of all the cultivated mushrooms.

½ cup mayonnaise

1 clove garlic, minced

2 tablespoons chopped fresh basil leaves

2 tablespoons olive oil

1 tablespoon balsamic vinegar

4 large portobello mushrooms, stems removed

Salt and coarsely ground black pepper to taste

Well-washed and torn spinach leaves, for topping

1. Mix together the mayonnaise, garlic, and basil in a small bowl. Set aside to let the flavors develop and use for topping.
2. In another small bowl, whisk together the olive oil and vinegar and brush over the mushrooms thoroughly. Season with salt and pepper.
3. Lightly oil the grill or a skillet over medium heat and cook the mushrooms until tender all the way through, 8 to 10 minutes per side.

SERVE IT UP on toasted *ciabatta* bread brushed with olive oil or in warm pita pockets

TOP IT OFF with a dollop of the basil mayonnaise and a handful of torn spinach leaves

WHO WOULD HAVE THOUGHT?

In 1981, Paul Wenner created the Gardenburger at his vegetarian restaurant in Gresham, Oregon. His veggie patty was so successful that he eventually shut down the restaurant to produce Gardenburgers for national distribution.

MUSHROOM GOAT CHEESE BURGERS WITH SUN-DRIED TOMATO CHUTNEY

MAKES 6 BURGERS

Duxelles **is the classic French mixture of chopped mushrooms and shallots cooked down and used for sauces and stuffings. It's delicious—rich in flavor and texture. Here we pair it with the "barnyardy" tartness of goat cheese. Make sure all the liquid from the mushrooms evaporates so your burgers don't fall apart.**

2 tablespoons olive oil

½ cup minced shallots

1 pound cremini or shiitake mushrooms, finely chopped

⅓ cup dry white wine

1 tablespoon chopped fresh thyme leaves

1 teaspoon salt

½ teaspoon coarsely ground black pepper

2 ounces goat cheese, crumbled

1. Preheat the oven to 350°F.
2. Heat the olive oil in a large skillet over medium-high heat. Add the shallots and cook, stirring, until barely soft and translucent, 2 to 3 minutes. Add the mushrooms, wine, thyme, salt, and pepper and cook down, stirring occasionally, until all the liquid has evaporated, 12 to 15 minutes.
3. Remove from the heat and mix in the goat cheese. Form the mixture into 6 patties, each ½ inch thick. Place on a baking sheet and bake for 15 minutes.

SERVE IT UP on Italian bread or toasted sesame seed buns

TOP IT OFF with Sun-Dried Tomato Chutney (recipe follows)

Sun-Dried Tomato Chutney

MAKES 1 CUP

The sweet-and-sour flavor is a nice foil for the goat cheese.

1 tablespoon olive oil

1 small yellow onion, finely chopped

½ cup golden raisins, soaked in warm water for 10 minutes and drained

½ cup finely chopped sun-dried tomatoes

2 tablespoons finely chopped pitted black and green olives

1 tablespoon capers, drained

1 tablespoon sugar

2 teaspoons good-quality balsamic vinegar

¼ teaspoon salt

1. Heat the olive oil in a small saucepan over medium heat. Add the onion, and cook, stirring, until soft and translucent, 1 to 2 minutes. Add the raisins, sun-dried tomatoes, olives, capers, sugar, vinegar, and salt and cook over low to medium heat, stirring occasionally, until slightly thickened, about 10 minutes.
2. Let cool, cover tightly, and refrigerate until ready to serve.

ROYAL FUNGUS

The ancient Egyptians considered mushrooms the plant of immortality. Apparently, the pharaohs were so taken with the edible fungi that they declared them food for royalty only. Commoners weren't even allowed to touch them.

CAULIFLOWER CREMINI BURGERS WITH ORANGE BASIL SAUCE

MAKES 6 BURGERS

Cauliflower and mushrooms are the perfect partners in this surprisingly hearty veggie burger. You can make these patties a day ahead and bake them at the last minute. The emerald sauce, infused with citrus, adds drama to the plate.

2 tablespoons olive oil

1 medium-size head cauliflower, stems removed and florets cut into ½-inch pieces

½ cup dry white wine

1 medium-size yellow onion, finely chopped

10 ounces cremini mushrooms, stems removed and caps finely chopped

¼ cup chicken or vegetable broth

1¾ cups seasoned croutons or rosemary crackers ground to fine crumbs

2 large egg whites

½ teaspoon salt

¼ teaspoon coarsely ground black pepper

1. In a medium-size skillet, heat 1 tablespoon of the olive oil over medium-high heat. Add the cauliflower and cook, stirring, until it just begins to brown, 2 to 4 minutes. Add ¼ cup of the wine, cover, and cook over low heat until tender but not mushy, about 10 minutes. Transfer to a large mixing bowl.
2. Heat the remaining 1 tablespoon olive oil in the skillet over medium heat. Add the onion and cook, stirring, until translucent, 1 to 2 minutes. Add the mushrooms and the remaining ¼ cup wine and continue to cook until the mushrooms have cooked down and the liquid has evaporated, 10 to 12 minutes.

3. In a large mixing bowl, combine the mushrooms and onion, cauliflower, broth, crouton crumbs, egg whites, salt, and pepper. Using your hands, form the mixture into 6 patties, each ½ to ¾ inch thick, and place on a baking sheet. Let cool, then cover with plastic wrap and refrigerate for at least 1 hour.
4. Preheat the oven to 375°F. Bake the burgers until golden brown, about 30 minutes.

SERVE IT UP on thick slices of sourdough or multigrain bread

TOP IT OFF with Orange Basil Sauce (recipe follows)

Orange Basil Sauce

MAKES 1 CUP

This refreshing, citrusy sauce adds pizzazz to fish and veggie burgers.

2 cups tightly packed fresh basil leaves

Juice of 2 oranges (about ½ cup)

2 tablespoons whole-grain Dijon mustard

¼ teaspoon salt

¼ cup olive oil

Place the basil, orange juice, mustard, and salt in a food processor. With the machine running, slowly pour the olive oil through the feed tube and process until smooth and thick.

EGGPLANT PARMIGIANA BURGERS

MAKES 3 OR 4 BURGERS

These burgers offer the satisfyingly familiar taste of this classic Italian dish. We love Japanese bread crumbs, called panko, for their crispy lightness—no heavy breading here. Since we keep the binding crumbs and egg to a minimum, it's important to handle the patties gently so they hold their shape.

2 tablespoons olive oil

5 cups peeled and finely diced eggplant

1 teaspoon crushed dried thyme

½ teaspoon salt

¼ teaspoon coarsely ground black pepper

¼ cup freshly grated Parmesan cheese

1 large egg

½ cup panko (see Ingredient Sources, page 232) or plain dry bread crumbs

2 cups marinara or spaghetti sauce

3 or 4 slices mozzarella cheese (about 3 or 4 ounces)

1. Preheat the oven to 350°F.
2. Heat 1 tablespoon of the oil in a large skillet over medium-high heat. Add the eggplant, thyme, salt, and pepper. Reduce the heat to medium and cook, stirring constantly, until the eggplant cooks down, 5 to 8 minutes.
3. Transfer the eggplant to a medium-size mixing bowl. Add the Parmesan, egg, and bread crumbs and combine well. Form into 3 or 4 patties, each about ½ inch thick.

4. Heat the remaining 1 tablespoon oil in the pan over medium heat. Using a metal spatula, transfer the patties to the pan and cook for 10 to 15 minutes total, turning after a nice crust forms on the bottom. This ensures that your burger will hold together well.
5. Put the sauce in a baking pan large enough to hold the patties in a single layer. Add the patties and top each of them with a mozzarella slice. Bake until the cheese is melted and lightly browned, about 15 minutes.

SERVE IT UP on toasted Italian country bread or toasted sesame seed buns

TOP IT OFF with the pan sauce

BRUSSELS SPROUT, APPLE, AND WALNUT BURGERS

MAKES 4 BURGERS

Okay, Brussels sprouts never did it for you. And the notion of putting them in burgers doesn't compute. But we believe that you'll become a Brussels sprout convert once you put these to the test. These slightly crunchy patties pack the sweetness of the apple and dried apricots, the nuttiness of the walnuts, and the flavor of the sprouts. Topped with Dijon mustard, they are downright delicious.

3 tablespoons olive oil

3 cups finely chopped Brussels sprouts

½ teaspoon salt

½ teaspoon coarsely ground black pepper

1 small yellow onion, finely chopped

1 Granny Smith apple, peeled, cored, and finely chopped (about 1½ cups)

½ cup ground walnuts

½ cup finely chopped dried apricots

½ cup plain dry bread crumbs

2 large eggs

1. Heat 1 tablespoon of the oil in a large skillet over medium-high heat. Add the Brussels sprouts, salt, and pepper. Reduce the heat to medium and cook, stirring constantly, until softened, 5 to 7 minutes. Transfer to a large mixing bowl.
2. Heat 1 tablespoon of the oil in a medium-size skillet over medium-high heat, add the onion, reduce the heat to medium, and cook, stirring, until translucent, 1 to 2 minutes. Add the apple and continue to cook, stirring frequently, until softened, 3 to 5 minutes.

3. Add the onion-apple mixture to the sprouts, then add the nuts, apricots, bread crumbs, and eggs and combine well. Compress the mixture tightly with your hands to form 4 patties, each ½ inch thick.
4. Heat the remaining 1 tablespoon oil in a large skillet over medium-high heat and cook the burgers until lightly browned, 3 to 5 minutes per side.

SERVE IT UP in warm pita pockets

TOP IT OFF with Dijon mustard

I WANT I YAM WHAT I YAM!

Indiana burger joint Googie's is famous for its toppings. Among its exotic burger offerings are the Maui (pineapple, onion, and bacon), the Kingston (peppers, carrots, and jerk sauce), and the I Yam What I Yam (sautéed spinach and feta).

Googie's Gourmet Burgers • 8487 Union Chapel Road • Indianapolis, IN 46240
(317) 202-9700 • www.gottagettagoogie.com

JALAPEÑO, ARTICHOKE, AND CORN BURGERS WITH CILANTRO CREAM SAUCE

MAKES 6 BURGERS

It's the creamy corn flavor that makes this burger the ultimate vegetarian comfort food. The patties start off as a batter in the skillet but finish off in the oven. The Cilantro Cream Sauce dresses this veggie burger in a bright green mantle of flavor.

One 1-pound bag frozen corn kernels (3 cups)

One 14-ounce can artichoke hearts, drained and quartered

1 large egg

1 cup panko (see Ingredient Sources, page 232) or plain dry bread crumbs

½ cup seeded and minced fresh jalapeño chile peppers

½ small red onion, minced

¼ teaspoon salt

2 tablespoons olive oil

1. Preheat the oven to 325°F.
2. In a food processor, combine the corn and artichokes and process until pulpy, scraping down the sides. Add the egg and ½ cup of the bread crumbs and pulse to combine. Transfer to a large mixing bowl. Mix in the jalapeños, red onion, salt, and remaining ½ cup bread crumbs.
3. Heat 1 tablespoon of the olive oil in a medium-size skillet over medium-high heat. Drop in three ¼ cupfuls of the batter mixture, using a spoon to shape into ½-inch-thick disks. Cook until a nice crust forms, 3 to 5 minutes. Flip and cook until the other side is crisp, about 3 minutes.

4. Drain on paper towels and place on a baking sheet. Repeat with the remaining 3 burgers. Place all 6 patties in the oven and bake for 30 minutes.

SERVE IT UP on thinly sliced whole wheat toast

TOP IT OFF with Cilantro Cream Sauce (recipe follows) and sliced tomato

Cilantro Cream Sauce

MAKES ABOUT 1 CUP

1 cup tightly packed fresh cilantro leaves

1 cup well-washed and torn spinach leaves (preferably baby spinach)

3 tablespoons crème fraîche or sour cream

¼ cup plus 2 tablespoons milk

¼ teaspoon coarsely ground black pepper

½ teaspoon salt

1. Place all the ingredients in a food processor and process until smooth.
2. Refrigerate for at least 1 hour, or up to overnight, to let the flavors develop.

BURGERS ON PARADE

The state of Wisconsin claims to be "Home of the Hamburger." In 1885, an enterprising teenager there flattened meatballs into burgers and put them between 2 slices of bread. Now Seymour, Wisconsin, holds an annual Burger Fest in August, with a ketchup slide, bun toss, and hamburger-eating contest, as well as the "world's largest hamburger parade."

ASIAN SALAD BURGERS

MAKES 6 BURGERS

At some time in your life, you've probably eaten stir-fried veggies served with rice and teriyaki sauce. Now imagine packing all that into a burger spiced with ginger. Easy and delicious, these burgers are filled with carrot and snow peas and served wrapped in frilly lettuce leaves. Serve with extra teriyaki sauce.

3 tablespoons canola oil

½ cup peeled and finely chopped fresh ginger

1 cup finely chopped carrot

1 cup finely chopped scallions (white and green parts)

½ cup drained and finely chopped water chestnuts

1 cup finely chopped snow peas

1 tablespoon teriyaki sauce

2 cups cooked short-grain white rice (see Note, page 127)

2 large eggs, lightly beaten

1. Heat 1 tablespoon of the oil in a skillet over medium-high heat. Add the ginger and stir-fry for 1 minute. Add the carrot and scallions and stir-fry for 1 minute. Add the water chestnuts, snow peas, and teriyaki sauce and stir-fry for 1 minute more. Transfer the mixture to a large mixing bowl.
2. Add the rice and eggs and combine well. To make the burgers, pack one-sixth of the mixture into a ½-cup measure and place the patty on a baking sheet. Repeat with the remaining mixture. Cover with plastic wrap and refrigerate for at least 30 minutes to firm up.

3. Heat 1 tablespoon of the oil in a large skillet over medium heat. Place 3 of the burgers in the pan and cook until a crust forms, about 3 minutes per side. Repeat with the remaining 3 burgers.

SERVE IT UP wrapped in large lettuce leaves, such as red leaf lettuce

TOP IT OFF with a splash of teriyaki sauce (or serve with a bowl of sauce for dipping)

GUINNESS RECORD TIME

The largest carrot recorded (in October 1990) was 193¼ inches.

DILLED CHICKPEA BURGERS WITH SPICY YOGURT SAUCE

MAKES 4 BURGERS

Dill and garlic is a classic Turkish flavor combination. For this healthy but filling burger, make the hot, garlicky yogurt sauce first so the spices have time to mingle. A cucumber salad and minted iced tea round out a light but satisfying lunch.

One 15-ounce can chickpeas, rinsed and well drained

⅓ cup chopped fresh dill

½ cup minced shallots

2 tablespoons plain dry bread crumbs

2 tablespoons fresh lemon juice

2 tablespoons tahini (sesame paste)

½ teaspoon salt

¼ teaspoon coarsely ground black pepper

¼ teaspoon ground cumin

1. Lightly mash half the chickpeas in a medium-size mixing bowl. Add the dill, shallots, bread crumbs, and lemon juice and mix well.
2. In a food processor, combine the remaining chickpeas, the tahini, salt, pepper, and cumin and process until smooth. Add to the mashed chickpeas and mix well. Form into 4 patties, each ½ inch thick.
3. Lightly oil the grill or a skillet over medium heat and cook the burgers until crispy and golden on both sides, about 5 minutes per side.

SERVE IT UP in warm pita pockets

TOP IT OFF with Spicy Yogurt Sauce (recipe follows) and sliced tomato

Spicy Yogurt Sauce

MAKES 1 CUP

1 cup plain nonfat yogurt

2 large cloves garlic, minced

½ teaspoon curry powder

¼ teaspoon cayenne pepper

Mix together all the ingredients in a small bowl.

WHERE KETCHUP IS TABOO

This New Haven landmark boasts that it invented the hamburger sandwich. Even the Library of Congress supports this claim, saying that Louis, at his original lunch wagon operation, ground leftover beef from the lunch rush, cooked it, and served it up between two slices of bread. Louis' Lunch continues to draw crowds at its present location, where ketchup is still taboo. (Louis's grandson, who runs the place today, maintains that it hides the flavor of the burger.) Onion, cheese, and tomato are the only topping options.

Louis' Lunch • 261–263 Crown Street • New Haven, CT 06510 • (203) 562-5507

www.louislunch.com

FALAFEL BURGERS

MAKES 6 BURGERS

These chickpea burgers originated in Egypt, where today they are still a popular snack. They are usually deep-fried, but the good news here is that there's much less fat, since these virtually sear in a thin coating of olive oil. Feel free to stuff extra vegetables such as slivered carrot, diced cucumber, sliced red onion—whatever your pleasure—into your pitas along with the burgers.

One 15-ounce can chickpeas, rinsed and well drained

3 cloves garlic, minced

2 teaspoons ground cumin

½ cup tightly packed fresh flat-leaf parsley leaves

½ cup tightly packed fresh cilantro leaves

1 tablespoon fresh lemon juice

3 tablespoons olive oil

½ medium-size yellow onion, finely chopped

3 tablespoons seeded and finely chopped fresh jalapeño chile peppers

1 large egg

½ teaspoon salt

¼ teaspoon coarsely ground black pepper

1. In a food processor, pulse the chickpeas, garlic, cumin, parsley, cilantro, lemon juice, and 1 tablespoon of the oil together just until a thick paste forms. Transfer the mixture to a large mixing bowl. Add the onion, jalapeños, egg, salt, and pepper and combine well. Form into 6 firm, flat patties, each about ½ inch thick.

2. Over medium-high heat, heat 1 tablespoon of the oil in a medium-size skillet. Add 3 of the patties to the pan and cook until golden brown, 2 to 4 minutes per side. Transfer to paper towels to drain. Repeat with the remaining 3 patties.

SERVE IT UP in warm pita pockets

TOP IT OFF with lettuce, sliced tomato, and a dollop of hummus

CARHOPS ARE HISTORY, BUT MEL'S ISN'T

This San Francisco burger institution started life as a drive-in with carhops. Today the carhops and tray clamps are gone, but customers keep streaming in. We hear the Melburger is still a favorite, but now there's also a list of veggie burgers to choose from.

Mel's Drive-In • 2165 Lombard Street at Fillmore Street
San Francisco, CA 94123 • (415) 921-2867
www.melsdrive-in.com

CHILI CHICKPEA FRITTER BURGERS WITH CURRIED YOGURT

MAKES 4 BURGERS

These are fried crispy golden like potato pancakes, except that we make them with chickpeas, also known as garbanzo beans. The earthy chickpeas get a shot in the arm from the fiery Thai chili paste, while the yogurt topping adds a cool finish.

One 15-ounce can chickpeas, rinsed and well drained

2 teaspoons Thai roasted red chili paste (see Ingredient Sources, page 232)

¼ cup all-purpose flour

1 large egg

1 teaspoon salt

¼ cup milk

¼ cup canola oil

1. Put all the ingredients except the canola oil in a blender and process until smooth. Transfer to a medium-size mixing bowl.
2. Heat the canola oil in a large skillet over medium-high heat. Pour 4 large ladlefuls of the chickpea mixture into the skillet, using up all the mixture. Cook for 4 to 5 minutes, until a crust forms. Gently turn over with a metal spatula and continue to cook. After the second side begins to crisp, carefully drain most of the oil out of the pan and reduce the heat to low. Cook for about 5 minutes more, until cooked through. Transfer to paper towels to drain.

SERVE IT UP in warm whole wheat pita pockets

TOP IT OFF with Curried Yogurt (recipe follows) and well-washed and torn spinach leaves

Curried Yogurt

MAKES 1 CUP

Thinned out with a bit of water, this makes a tasty salad dressing.

1 tablespoon curry powder

1 cup plain lowfat yogurt

Add the curry powder to the yogurt and mix well.

SPICY BLACK BEAN BURGERS

MAKES 4 BURGERS

It's chips, dip, and salsa all rolled into one in this southwestern-flavored burger. We use crushed tortilla chips to literally hold it all together. The result? A burger so tasty that even die-hard carnivores will love it.

Two 15-ounce cans black beans, rinsed and well drained

1 small red onion, diced

½ cup seeded and diced green bell pepper

½ cup finely crushed tortilla chips

½ cup chopped fresh cilantro leaves

1 tablespoon chili powder

1 teaspoon ground cumin

½ teaspoon red pepper flakes

2 teaspoons canola oil

1. Mash the beans in a large mixing bowl. Add the onion, bell pepper, tortilla chips, cilantro, chili powder, cumin, and red pepper flakes and mix well. Shape into 4 patties, each 1 inch thick.
2. Heat the oil in a large skillet over medium-high heat and cook the burgers until crisp on the outside, 2 to 4 minutes per side.

SERVE IT UP on toasted sesame seed buns or in warm pita pockets

TOP IT OFF with shredded pepper Jack cheese and Rick Bayless's Roasted Jalapeño Tomato Salsa (page 123)

ZAMAR GUT GUT BURGERS WITH BULGUR, CUMIN, AND SCALLIONS

MAKES 4 TO 6 SERVINGS

Jane created these burgers based on a recipe she's been making for more than 20 years. It's written on a faded index card with lots of drips and stains. The ex-girlfriend of someone she used to know gave it to her. She has no idea what *zamar* and *gut gut* mean, but we think they sound Middle Eastern or Moroccan. Anyway, each spicy, grain-based burger is wrapped in curly edged red leaf lettuce. These festive packets with their intense flavors are ideal for parties.

1 cup fine-grind bulgur wheat

½ cup olive oil

One 6-ounce can tomato paste

3 scallions (white and green parts), finely chopped

¼ cup sweet paprika

¼ cup ground cumin

½ teaspoon salt

½ teaspoon coarsely ground black pepper

Red leaf lettuce leaves

1. Mix all the ingredients together in a large mixing bowl, cover with plastic wrap, and let sit all day or overnight in the refrigerator. This is important; the bulgur needs time to soften.
2. Form heaping tablespoonfuls of the mixture into small patties, pressing them tightly by hand.
3. Wrap each patty in a lettuce leaf.

SERVE IT UP by stuffing 2 or 3 packets into a warm pita pocket

TOP IT OFF with hummus

QUINOA AND MUSHROOM BURGERS

MAKES 6 BURGERS

Anita Pepper Kavanaugh, a good friend of Jane's daughter Caitie, raves about this recipe, which she first tasted while studying abroad in South America. She was in the Intag Cloud Forest Reserve in northwestern Ecuador, which is run by a couple who are "eco-warriors" with sophisticated palates. Anita graciously sent us the recipe, and we played around with it, adding shiitake mushrooms and cilantro for flavor and color. We wish we could have gone along on her trek through this exotic Eden, but at least the burgers made their way to us.

3 tablespoons olive oil

½ cup finely chopped leeks (white part only)

1 cup tightly packed chopped shiitake mushroom caps

1 cup cooked long-grain white rice

2 cups cooked quinoa (see Note)

½ cup rolled oats

6 cloves garlic, minced

¾ cup grated carrot

1 cup grated mozzarella cheese

2 large eggs, lightly beaten

1 tablespoon soy sauce

1 tablespoon Asian chili garlic sauce

¼ cup tightly packed chopped fresh cilantro leaves

1. Heat 1 tablespoon of the oil in a medium-size skillet over medium-high heat. Add the leeks and mushrooms and cook, stirring constantly, until just softened, about 1 minute. Transfer to a large mixing bowl.

2. Add the rice, quinoa, oats, garlic, carrot, cheese, eggs, soy sauce, chili sauce, and cilantro to the mushroom mixture. Using your hands, combine well. Form into 6 patties, each 1 inch thick. Cover with plastic wrap and refrigerate for at least 30 minutes to firm up.
3. Heat 1 tablespoon of the oil in a large skillet over medium-high heat. Reduce the heat to medium, add 3 of the burgers, and cook until a golden brown crust forms on the bottom, 3 to 4 minutes. Flip and continue to cook for 5 minutes more. Repeat with the remaining 3 burgers.

NOTE **To cook the quinoa, heat 1 tablespoon olive oil in a large pot over medium heat. Add 2 shallots, minced, and 2 cloves garlic, minced, and cook, stirring, until the onion is translucent, about 1 minute. Add 2 cups rinsed quinoa and cook, stirring a few times, for 2 minutes. Add 3 cups water and ½ teaspoon salt. Cover, reduce the heat to medium-low, and simmer until the water is absorbed and the quinoa is tender, about 25 minutes. Makes 4½ cups, more than you'll need for this burger recipe. Use the leftover quinoa in a salad with chopped scallions, radishes, currants, and almonds, all tossed with a nice vinaigrette.**

SERVE IT UP on Honey Whole Wheat with Seeds from Amy's Bread (page 218) or wrapped in warm flour tortillas

TOP IT OFF with sliced ripe avocado and Dijon mustard or Tomato Mint Chutney (page 76)

DYE JOBS

In the Middle Ages, dairy farmers added carrot juice to butter to give it a more appetizing color.

TOFU WALNUT CROQUETTE BURGERS ON AMY'S BREAD

MAKES 6 BURGERS

Deborah Madison, celebrated author of *The Greens Cookbook* and other cherished vegetarian cookbooks, contributed this satisfying veggie burger. She suggests that if you prefer a denser texture than the light and fluffy patties this recipe produces, replace the bread crumbs with bulgur or cooked brown rice. Deborah also advises pressing the tofu before using it, to eliminate the excess moisture. Wrap these delicious nut-flavored creations in Amy Scherber's Honey Whole Wheat with Seeds, and you've got yourself a winner.

One 12-ounce package firm tofu, drained

1 tablespoon olive oil

1 large onion, finely diced

¼ cup finely chopped fresh marjoram leaves or 2½ teaspoons dried

1½ teaspoons finely chopped fresh thyme leaves or ½ teaspoon dried

8 ounces cremini mushrooms, finely chopped

2 teaspoons Worcestershire sauce

1 to 2 tablespoons soy sauce, to your taste

2 large cloves garlic, minced or pressed

1 cup unsalted dry-roasted walnuts or cashews, finely ground

1 cup panko (see Ingredient Sources, page 232) or plain dry bread crumbs

1½ teaspoons Dijon mustard

Salt and coarsely ground black pepper to taste

1 large egg, lightly beaten

1. Wrap the tofu in a clean kitchen towel and place it on a cutting board tilted toward the sink. Place a heavy object on top and let it drain while you prepare everything else.
2. Heat the oil in a large skillet over medium-high heat. Add the onion, marjoram, and thyme. Cover and cook, stirring a few times, for 5 minutes. Add the mushrooms, increase the heat to high, and cook, stirring more frequently, until the mushrooms have given off and reabsorbed any liquid, about 8 minutes. Add the Worcestershire, soy sauce, and garlic and stir rapidly for about 1 minute, taking special care not to burn the garlic. (Remove the pan from the heat if that threatens to happen.)
3. Scrape the onion-mushroom mixture into a large mixing bowl. Add the ground nuts, bread crumbs, and mustard and combine well.
4. Crumble the tofu into the skillet and cook, stirring, over high heat until lightly colored but still tender to the touch, about 3 minutes. Season with salt and pepper, then add to the onion mixture. Taste for seasoning; you may need to add more salt, pepper, mustard, or soy sauce to bring the flavors up to where you want them, and you'll want to do that before adding the egg.
5. Add the egg and mix well. Divide the mixture into 6 equal portions and shape into rounds or ovals, each ¾ inch thick.
6. Lightly brush a large skillet with olive oil, then fry the croquettes over medium heat until golden, carefully turning them once with a spatula, 6 to 8 minutes total.

SERVE IT UP on lightly toasted Honey Whole Wheat with Seeds from Amy's Bread (page 218)

TOP IT OFF with Dijon mustard, mayonnaise, lettuce, and sliced tomato

AN ACCIDENTAL SAUCE

Chemists John Lea and William Perrins were onto something big when they mistakenly left a vegetable and fish mixture down in the basement for 2 years. The aged mixture became known as Worcestershire sauce, which was advertised to make "your hair grow beautiful."

Honey Whole Wheat with Seeds from Amy's Bread

MAKES ONE 2-POUND LOAF

Amy Scherber's inspired loaves enhance Manhattan's breadbaskets. Here her slightly crunchy, ever-so-sweet whole wheat creation offers burger lovers a choice wrap for their two-fisted meals. Amy loves grainy breads and is committed to using organic ingredients whenever possible. We think Amy's whole wheat treatment is especially good with veggie patties such as Deborah Madison's Tofu Walnut Croquette Burgers. Don't be intimidated by the steps; the recipe comes together rather easily.

1 teaspoon active dry yeast

¼ cup very warm water (105° to 115°F)

1¼ cups cool water (75°F)

1½ cups Sponge Starter (page 220)

3 tablespoons honey

1½ cups unbleached all-purpose flour

2 cups organic whole wheat flour (preferably coarse ground)

1 tablespoon plus 1 teaspoon kosher salt

½ cup sesame seeds

1 tablespoon flax seeds (see Ingredient Sources, page 231)

1 tablespoon millet seeds (see Ingredient Sources, page 231)

1. Combine the yeast and warm water in a large mixing bowl and stir with a fork to dissolve the yeast. Let stand until bubbly, about 3 minutes.
2. Add the cool water, sponge starter, and honey and mix with your fingers for 2 minutes, breaking up the sponge. This mixture should look milky and slightly foamy. Add the flours, salt, and seeds and mix with your fingers to incorporate, scraping the sides of the bowl and folding the dough over itself until it gathers into a mass. The dough will be somewhat sticky.

3. Transfer the dough to a lightly floured work surface and knead for about 5 minutes, using as little additional flour as possible. The dough should still feel slightly sticky. Sprinkle a little flour on the work surface and mound the dough into a ball. Cover the dough with oiled plastic wrap and let rest for 20 minutes.

4. After the rest period, knead the dough again for another minute. Shape the dough into a loose ball and place in a lightly oiled bowl, turning the dough to coat the top with oil. Cover the bowl tightly with plastic wrap and let rise at room temperature (75° to 77°F) for 1 to 2 hours, until the dough looks puffy and has nearly doubled in volume.

5. Gently dump the dough onto a lightly floured surface. Pat it gently into a rectangle about 12 inches long, 8 inches wide, and 1½ to 2 inches thick. Now fold the dough as you would an envelope: fold the top third down to the middle. Then fold the bottom third up to the middle. Turn this rectangle one-quarter turn and fold the top down and the bottom up again. Now turn this small rectangle into a log by rolling the top edge down by a third, sealing the seam with the edge of your hand, rolling it down a third more and sealing, and finally rolling it over the rest of the way and sealing tightly. Place the log seam side down in a lightly oiled 9 x 5-inch loaf pan. Cover with oiled plastic wrap and let rise at room temperature for 1 to 1½ hours, until the dough is nearly doubled in size and domes slightly over the top of the pan.

6. Thirty minutes before baking, preheat the oven to 450°F. Make sure the top oven rack is placed a third of the way from the bottom of the oven so the loaf doesn't brown too much on top.

7. Gently place the pan on the top rack and quickly mist the loaf 8 to 10 times using a spray bottle filled with water. Shut the oven door, then mist again after 1 minute. Bake for 15 minutes, reduce the oven temperature to 375°F, and bake for 20 to 25 minutes more, until the crust is a deep brown color and the loaf sounds hollow when removed from the pan and tapped on the bottom. Remove the bread from the pan and cool on a wire rack.

Sponge Starter

1½ cups very warm water (105° to 115°F)

¼ teaspoon active dry yeast

3½ cups bleached all-purpose flour

1. Mix all the ingredients together in a medium-size mixing bowl. Stir them vigorously with a wooden spoon until a smooth, somewhat elastic dough forms, about 2 minutes. The sponge will be slightly stiff; it will get softer and more elastic after it rises.
2. Scrape the sponge into a glass or plastic bowl or container and cover it with plastic wrap. Mark the height of the starter and the time on a piece of tape on the side of the container so you can see how much it rises.
3. At this point you have 2 options: If you plan to make your dough later that same day, let the sponge rest at room temperature until it has risen to the point just before it begins to collapse. This may take 6 to 8 hours, depending on the temperature of the sponge, the temperature of the room, and the strength of the yeast. It will triple in size, and very small dents and folds will begin to appear in the top as it reaches its peak and begins to deflate. Use it before it collapses too much.

   If you're not planning to make your dough until the next day or the day after, put the covered sponge in the refrigerator and let it rise there for at least 14 hours before taking it out to use in a recipe. Be sure to compensate for the cold temperature of the starter by using warm water (85° to 90°F) in the dough instead of the cool water specified in the recipe. Or let the sponge sit out, covered, until it reaches room temperature (this may take several hours), but don't let it collapse before using it.

RED, WHITE, AND BLUE TOFU BURGERS

MAKES 4 BURGERS

This vegetarian burger is as patriotic as you can get—red onion and beets, white tofu, and blue cheese. Together, the subtle and strong flavors create a perfect balance: the sweet beets and creamy tofu offset the pungent onion and blue cheese.

One 12-ounce package firm tofu, well drained and mashed

1 small red onion, finely chopped

1 clove garlic, minced

1 large egg, lightly beaten

½ cup plain dry bread crumbs

½ teaspoon salt

½ teaspoon coarsely ground black pepper

1 tablespoon olive oil

1. Mix together all the ingredients except the olive oil in a medium-size mixing bowl. Form into 4 patties, each about ½ inch thick.
2. Heat the olive oil in a large nonstick skillet over medium heat and cook the burgers until golden brown on both sides, 3 to 5 minutes per side.

SERVE IT UP on toasted sesame seed buns

TOP IT OFF with thinly sliced cooked beets, thinly sliced red onion, and crumbled blue cheese

CARROT MUSHROOM TOFU BURGERS

MAKES 4 BURGERS

Forget those frozen patties that taste like cardboard. These veggie burgers redefine tofu, redolent as they are with ginger, garlic, and sesame. Just be sure to extract as much water as possible from the tofu so the burgers hold together.

One 12-ounce package firm tofu, well drained

2 teaspoons canola oil

2 teaspoons peeled and minced fresh ginger

⅓ cup shredded carrot

¼ cup finely diced shiitake mushrooms

¼ cup thinly sliced scallions (white and green parts)

2 cloves garlic, minced

1½ tablespoons soy sauce

2 large egg whites, lightly beaten

1½ teaspoons toasted sesame oil

½ cup ground rolled oats (ground in a food processor)

1. Place the tofu in a food processor and pulse until coarsely chopped. Remove and place in a double layer of cheesecloth or a clean kitchen towel. Gather the ends together and twist tightly, squeezing out as much water as possible. Do this a couple of times.
2. Remove the tofu from the cheesecloth and place in a medium-size mixing bowl.
3. In a large nonstick skillet, heat ½ teaspoon of the canola oil over medium heat. Add the ginger and cook, stirring, for 1 minute. Add the carrot, mushrooms, scallions, and garlic and cook, stirring, until just softened, 2 to 4 minutes.

4. Add the carrot mixture, soy sauce, egg whites, sesame oil, and ground oats to the tofu and mix well. Taste and adjust the seasonings. Form into 4 patties, each ½ inch thick.
5. In the same skillet over medium heat, heat the remaining 1½ teaspoons canola oil. Add the burgers and cook until golden brown on both sides, 2 to 4 minutes per side.

SERVE IT UP on toasted whole wheat buns

TOP IT OFF with grated cheddar cheese or Green Dijon Sauce (page 139)

WHAT'S UP, DOC?

Carrots were originally considered a medicine. Ancient Greek doctors used the roots and juice to treat indigestion, snakebites, and even cancer.

Ingredient Glossary

ADOBO SAUCE This spicy red sauce is made from chile peppers, spices, and vinegar and is often used as a marinade for chipotle chiles. Don't confuse it with adobo, a pork and chicken dish from the Philippines.

ANDOUILLE SAUSAGE Pronounced on-DOO-wee, this smoky, spicy pork sausage is a defining flavor in Cajun cooking. Used in gumbo and jambalaya, it's worth the effort to find (see Ingredient Sources), but if you can't get it, use Polish kielbasa instead.

BOK CHOY Also known as Chinese white cabbage, bok choy has long white stalks and dark green leaves. It has a mild flavor and is often used in stir-fries.

BULGUR This Middle Eastern wheat staple comes in different grinds: coarse, medium, and fine. It also is available whole or cracked. Bulgur can be mixed with oils and sauces or cooked like rice. Its chewy texture and nutlike flavor are featured in tabbouleh, a popular grain salad.

CERIGNOLA OLIVES These giant, bright green olives come from the Adriatic coast of southern Italy. Mild and sweet, with a very solid "meaty" flesh, they are preserved in brine or vinegar.

CHICKEN GLACE Pronounced glahs, this is a rich chicken stock that has been reduced to a thick, syrupy consistency, chicken glace adds body and flavor to sauces. If you can't find it locally, order it online (see Ingredient Sources).

CHILE PEPPERS

Anaheim: This mild green chile has a long, skinny shape and is commonly used in salsas.

Chipotle: Pronounced chee-POTE-lay, this exotic-sounding chile is actually a smoked jalapeño. It is dried and has a deep, sweet flavor and a bit of heat. You can also find chipotles canned in adobo sauce.

Jalapeño: Pronounced ha-lah-PAIN-yo, this small, smooth, green chile measures about 2 inches long and 1 inch wide. It is usually medium hot to very hot.

New Mexico green chile: The young version of the long, skinny New Mexico red chile, it has a mild flavor and is often used in southwestern cooking.

Poblano: This green-black chile has a rich, smoky flavor. Dried poblanos are called ancho chiles.

Scotch bonnet: One of the hottest chiles around, this small chile ranges in color from yellow-orange to red.

Serrano: This small yellow chile is very hot.

CHINESE FIVE-SPICE POWDER A staple in Chinese cooking, made of equal parts ground cinnamon, cloves, fennel seeds, star anise, and Szechuan peppercorns, it's available in Asian markets and most supermarkets.

CRÈME FRAÎCHE This thick, velvety cream with a slight tang originated in France. You can find it in supermarkets or make your own, as follows: Mix 1 cup heavy cream with 2 tablespoons buttermilk and let stand at room temperature until very thick, at least 8 hours or up to 1 day. Stir before covering. Keep refrigerated.

DAIKON This large Oriental radish gets its name from the Japanese words *dai* (large) and *kon* (root). It's crispy, juicy, and refreshing, with a subtle sweetness, and its skin can be white or black. Measuring anywhere from 6 to 15 inches long and 2 to 3 inches in diameter, it's an imposing addition to the shopping cart. It can be found year-round in most supermarkets.

FALAFEL The familiar version of these Middle Eastern croquettes are shaped like balls and made from highly spiced ground chickpeas. The most popular accompaniments are yogurt- or tahini-based sauces, such as hummus, and pita bread or lavash.

FISH SAUCE A clear brown liquid that is very pungent and salty, this is a key flavor in Southeast Asian cooking. Made from fermented anchovies, fish sauce can be off-putting, but the flavor mellows once it's cooked. It's commonly found in Asian markets. There is no adequate substitute—soy sauce won't cut it.

GARAM MASALA This Indian blend, composed of warming spices such as cinnamon, black pepper, cloves, cumin, and cardamom, is available in Indian markets.

GRAPE LEAVES Often used in Mediterranean cooking, grape leaves give a briny flavor to the food they're wrapped around. They're immersed in liquid and sold in jars.

HEARTS OF PALM The inner parts of the cabbage palm tree, they're sold in cans in many supermarkets. Mild-flavored, hearts of palm are cream colored and look like white asparagus stalks.

HERBES DE PROVENCE This mixture of dried herbs commonly found in the south of France may include lavender, thyme, basil, and marjoram. You can usually find it in the spice section of most supermarkets.

HOISIN SAUCE A thick, soybean-based brown sauce, hoisin is very popular in Chinese cooking. It is both sweet and savory and is also used as a dipping sauce. Commonly found in the Asian foods section of the supermarket, it's sometimes called Peking sauce.

***MOO SHU* PANCAKES** These thin Chinese pancakes are similar to flour tortillas and are a familiar accompaniment to dishes such as Peking duck and *moo shu* pork. You can find them in Asian markets and most large supermarkets.

OYSTER SAUCE This dark brown sauce made from oysters and soy sauce is boiled down until it's thick. Used frequently in Chinese cooking, oyster sauce gives depth and richness to dishes while enhancing the natural flavor of the ingredients.

PANKO These Japanese bread crumbs are lighter than typical dry bread crumbs. When properly pan-fried, they have a wonderfully light, crispy, greaseless texture.

QUENELLE A delicate, oval dumpling made of seasoned minced or ground protein and a binder such as flour, bread crumbs, or rice mixed with water, stock, milk, butter, or egg yolk. Spoons are used to form each *quenelle*, and the dumplings are then poached in stock or wine and served with a rich sauce.

QUINOA Pronounced KEEN-wah, this is a South American grain that is similar to millet. Quinoa has the most protein of any grain and cooks up like rice. It is available in many supermarkets and most health food stores.

SHISO This aromatic herb is part of the mint family. Sometimes called Japanese basil or perilla, it is available in Asian markets. If you can't find shiso, substitute basil or mint.

TAHINI Tahini is a paste made from ground sesame seeds. It also can refer to a sauce made from tahini paste. Tahini is used in hummus and can be kept at room temperature. It's sold in many supermarkets and in Middle Eastern markets.

WASABI Also known as Japanese horseradish, wasabi is a pale green condiment that comes as a powder or paste. It has a sharp, hot flavor and is typically mixed with soy sauce and eaten with sushi and sashimi. The powder has a much longer shelf life than the paste and can be turned into paste simply by adding water.

Ingredient Sources

ANDOUILLE SAUSAGE

Many grocers and other online sources carry this product.

Cajun Market of New Orleans
(888) 43-CAJUN (432-2586)
www.cajunmarket.com

Pure Cajun Products
1103 Taylor Street
New Orleans, LA 70062
(800) 376-1039
www.purecajun.com

ASIAN GARLIC CHILI PASTE (OR PUREE)

You may also find this hot, spicy sauce in the Asian foods section of your supermarket.

China Bowl Trading Company
P.O. Box 454
Westport, CT 06881
(203) 222-0381

BUFFALO MEAT

Tender and sweet, buffalo meat is gaining in popularity because of its famously low fat content. Ask your local butcher, or contact the Jackson Hole Buffalo Meat Company in Wyoming.

Jackson Hole Buffalo Meat Company
P.O. Box 2100
1655 Berger Lane
Jackson, WY 83001
(800) 543-6328
www.jhbuffalomeat.com

CHICKEN GLACE

Glace de Poulet Gold provides pure, intense flavor when used to enhance finished sauces or when deglazing directly in a roasting or sauté pan.

Glace de Poulet Gold
More Than Gourmet
929 Home Avenue
Akron, OH 44310
(800) 860-9385
www.morethangourmet.com

CHINESE FIVE-SPICE POWDER

You can usually find this in the Asian foods section or in the spice aisle of your supermarket.

The Spice House
1031 North Old World Third Street
Milwaukee, WI 53203
(414) 272-0977
www.thespicehouse.com

CONCH

You can order whole or ground conch for next-day delivery.

Captain Ed's Lobster Trap
1901 South Federal Highway
Fort Lauderdale, FL 33316
(954) 522-5722

CRANBERRY HORSERADISH SAUCE

Stonewall Kitchen products are available in many supermarkets and gourmet shops, or you can order direct.

Stonewall Kitchen
Stonewall Lane
York, ME 03909
(800) 207-JAMS (5267)
www.stonewallkitchen.com

CRAWFISH

This tiny crustacean (also called crayfish or crawdad) is a classic ingredient in Cajun cooking.

Louisiana Cajun Crawfish
430 Hillary Street
New Orleans, LA 70118
(504) 461-8794
www.crawfishguy.com

Louisiana Crawfish Company
(888) 522-7292
www.lacrawfish.com

DUNGENESS CRAB

Get live crabs shipped to your door in season.

Leo's Live Seafood
4098 Legoe Bay Road
Lummi Island, WA 98262
(360) 758-7318
www.leoslive.com

Pure Food Fish Market
1515 Price Place
Seattle, WA 98101
(800) 392-FISH (3474)
www.freshseafood.com

FISH SAUCE

You probably won't find this pungent condiment at your local supermarket, so go online.

i-Clipse
4905 Morena Boulevard, Suite 1313
San Diego, CA 92117
(800) 910-WOKS (9657)
www.pacificrim-gourmet.com

Ethnicgrocer.com
162 West Hubbard Street, 3rd Floor
Chicago, IL 60601
(866) 4ETHNIC (438-4642)
www.ethnicgrocer.com

FLAX SEEDS

This healthful ingredient is available at most health food stores. Flax has become particularly popular now that we know it has a lot of those heart-healthy omega-3 fatty acids. If you have difficulty finding flax seeds, order online.

The Grain & Salt Society
273 Fairway Drive
Asheville, NC 28805
(800) 867-7258
www.saltoflife.com

GARAM MASALA

Ethnicgrocer.com (see Fish sauce)

The Spice Hunter
P.O. Box 8110
184 Suburban Road
San Luis Obispo, CA 93403
(800) 444-3061
www.spicehunter.com

HOISIN SAUCE

If you can't find this at the supermarket, order online.

Chefshop.com
P.O. Box 3488
1435 Elliott Avenue West
Seattle, WA 98114
(877) 337-2491
www.chefshop.com

MEAT

This Boston-area prime butcher offers some of the finest meats to be found.

John Dewar & Co.
753–755 Beacon Street
Newton Centre, MA 02459
(617) 964-3577
www.sorcerersolutions.com/JohnDewar.html

This high-end butcher is expensive but worth it, with beautiful-looking beef, lamb, veal, and pork. Lobel's also will special-order buffalo or ostrich meat.

Lobel's of New York
1096 Madison Avenue
New York, NY 10028
(877) 783-4512
www.lobels.com

MILLET SEEDS

If you can't find these at your local health food store, try Whole Foods Market (see next entry).

ORGANIC FOODS

With 133 outlets nationwide, this upscale grocer is known for its quality organic foods.

Whole Foods Market
601 North Lamar, Suite 300
Austin, TX 78703
(512) 477-4455
www.wholefoodsmarket.com

OSTRICH MEAT

Ostrich meat is slowly catching on as a healthful alternative to beef.

Ostrich Growers Meat Company
120 Shell Drive
Watsonville, CA 95076
(831) 722-4671
www.ostrichgrowers.com

OYSTER SAUCE

Ethnicgrocer.com (see Fish sauce)

PANKO

In addition to using them in these recipes, try them for fried chicken or breaded pork chops.

Ethnicgrocer.com (see Fish sauce)

PRODUCE

Boston-area shoppers flock to Russo's for quality produce at reasonable prices.

A. Russo and Sons
560 Pleasant Street
Watertown, MA 02472
(617) 923-1500
www.arusso.com

SEAFOOD

These two purveyors are among the finest on the East Coast.

Citarella
2135 Broadway
New York, NY 10023
1313 Third Avenue
New York, NY 10021
(212) 874-0383
www.citarella.com

Legal Sea Foods
33 Everett Street
Boston, MA 02134
(800) 343-5804
www.legalseafoods.com

THAI RED CURRY PASTE

THAI ROASTED RED CHILI PASTE

These concentrated blends are also available in many supermarkets and gourmet outlets.

Thai Kitchen
1919 Market Street, Suite 100
Oakland, CA 94607
(800) 967-THAI (8424)
www.thaikitchen.com

Acknowledgments

Like two actors at the Oscars, we can't begin without thanking our agent. Deborah Krasner is one terrific cheerleader. She devotedly sought the right home for this burger opus. Thanks, Deborah, for your enthusiastic support, humor, and ready accessibility.

Thanks to our editor at The Harvard Common Press, Pam Hoenig. Pam scrupulously combed through our recipes, helping with formatting and offering welcome suggestions along the way. We're lucky to have been the beneficiaries of her careful review and insightful input.

A bow to Barbara Jatkola, copyeditor extraordinaire, who invested so much in ensuring that every *t* was crossed and every *i* dotted.

Many thanks to Jane and Michael Stern and Stephen Rushmore, Jr., for their Web site, www.roadfood.com. It proved a valuable resource in researching burger joints across the country.

Our deep appreciation goes to Jackie Newgent, spokesperson for the American Dietetic Association, for her time and generosity in providing nutritional information.

We invited a select group of chefs and cookbook authors from around the country to each share a recipe from his or her repertoire for our burger bible. The following talents generously came through with the yummy offerings you'll find on our pages. Many thanks to:

Rick Bayless, for Roasted Jalapeño Tomato Salsa. Proponent of Mexico's regional cuisines, Rick has acquired a pantry full of kudos, including the James Beard Foundation's National Chef of the Year award and the Julia Child/IACP Best Cookbook of the Year award for his book *Authentic Mexican: Regional Cooking from the Heart of Mexico*. He is the chef/owner of the Frontera Grill and Topolobampo in Chicago and host of the PBS series *Mexico—One Plate at a Time*.

Norma Jean Darden, for North Carolina Chopped Barbecued Pork Burgers. Norma is the co-author of *Spoonbread and Strawberry Wine* and the owner of the southern-style restaurants Miss Maude's Spoonbread Too and Miss Mamie's Spoonbread Too in New York City, as well as of Spoonbread Catering.

Robert Del Grande, for Texas-Style Beef Burgers with Pinto Beans, Bacon, and Green Chiles. Executive chef and partner of Houston's acclaimed Cafe Annie and other eating ventures in Houston and Dallas, Robert has received many culinary awards and honors, including a James Beard Foundation award, *Food & Wine*'s Best Restaurant Houston award, and inclusion in *Gourmet*'s America's Top Tables.

Reed Hearon, for Rich Man's Hamburger. Reed is a chef, restaurant owner, and cookbook author, with degrees in math and philosophy and with three destination restaurants in San Francisco's North Beach area: Rose Pistola (winner of the James Beard Foundation Best New Restaurant award), Rose's Café, and Black Cat.

Legal Sea Foods executive chef Rich Vellante, for Legal Sea Foods Tuna Burgers. There are 26 Legal Sea Foods restaurants along the East Coast, from Massachusetts to Florida. Legal has a catalog and a Web site as well, so no matter where you live, you can order in a lobster clambake, even in the dead of winter.

Deborah Madison, for her Tofu Walnut Croquette Burgers. This celebrated cookbook author, winner of the Julia Child/IACP Best Cookbook of the Year award and a James Beard Foundation award, was the founding chef of Greens Restaurant in San Francisco, one of the foremost vegetarian dining spots in the country.

Laurie Paul, for Laurie's Dungeness Crab Burgers with Sweet Roasted Pepper Rouille. After years of cooking at the Friday Harbor House in Washington State's San Juan Islands, chef Laurie Paul has opened a catering and prepared foods shop, the Market Chef. Laurie, whose accolades include cooking at the James Beard House and praise from *Gourmet* and *Bon Appétit*, hopes to promote local artisan food as well.

Mark Peel and Nancy Silverton, for Mark Peel's Gorgonzola Hamburgers on Nancy Silverton's Hamburger Buns. This award-winning husband-and-wife chef and pastry chef are the owners of Campanile, one of L.A.'s most celebrated restaurants. Nancy is also proprietor of the La Brea Bakery, located both in Van Nuys and adjacent to the restaurant. Both have written a number of books, including *Nancy Silverton's Breads from the La Brea Bakery* and *The Food of Campanile*.

Steven Raichlen, for Bulgarian Burgers. This acclaimed author, food writer, and cooking teacher is a three-time winner of a Julia Child/IACP cookbook award for his books *Miami Spice*, *The Barbecue! Bible*, and *How to Grill*. He is also the author of *Barbecue! Bible Sauces, Rubs, and Marinades* and *Beer-Can Chicken*.

Amy Scherber, for Honey Whole Wheat with Seeds. The owner of Amy's Bread, with three Manhattan locations, Amy is also the coauthor of *Amy's Bread*.

Michael Schlow, for Late-Night Beef Burger with Cheddar, Horseradish, and Onion. Chef and co-owner of Boston's elegant dining sensation Radius, Michael was named a *Food & Wine* Best New Chef, and Radius was named *Food & Wine*'s Best New Restaurant 2000.

Arthur Schwartz, for Brooklyn Ketchup. Arthur is a newspaper food editor, restaurant critic (*New York Daily News*), host of the radio show *Food Talk* (heard daily on New York's WOR 710 AM radio), and author of numerous cookbooks.

Susan Spicer, for Crawfish Pork Burgers with Scallion Mayo. One of New Orleans's premier chefs, with three restaurants, Susan has a roster of awards to her credit, including *Food & Wine*'s Best New Chef, the James Beard Foundation's Best Chef: Southeast, and the Robert Mondavi Culinary Award of Excellence.

Ming Tsai and Terrence Maul, for Tuna Shiso Burgers with Asian Salsa. Ming Tsai is chef/owner of the Blue Ginger restaurant in Wellesley, Massachusetts. Terrence Maul is his sous chef. Ming is also host of *East Meets West with Ming Tsai* on the Food Network and author of the cookbook *Blue Ginger*.

Norman Van Aken, for Barbecued Ropa Vieja Burgers with Escabeche Spice Rub That Cures. Norman has been hailed by the *New York Times* as South Florida's "most gifted chef." He is a past winner of the James Beard Foundation's Best Chef: Southeast award and has also received the Robert Mondavi Award and the Food Arts Silver Spoon award for lifetime achievement. He is the author of four cookbooks, and his restaurant, Norman's, was listed by the Zagat Survey as the best restaurant in Miami and by *Condé Nast Traveler* as one of its top 10 restaurants in the United States.

Jonathan Waxman, for Jonathan Waxman's Hamburgers. Jonathan shot to fame when he brought California cuisine to New York with his groundbreaking restaurant, Jams. A huge believer in fresh, seasonal ingredients prepared simply, his latest venture is Washington Park, which has opened to critical acclaim.

Trevor White, for Fog City Grilled Lamb Burgers with Tomato Mint Chutney and Roasted Bell Pepper Chow-Chow. Executive chef of Fog City since 2001, Trevor is a graduate of the California Culinary Academy and has trained under noted San Francisco chef and fellow burger contributor Reed Hearon.

Index